NET WORTH

DEAN WALKER

NET WORTH
The memories of C.E. Pickering

YORKMINSTER PUBLISHING • TORONTO

Copyright © December 1973 by Dean Walker

All rights reserved. No part of this publication may be reproduced, stored in a retrieval system, or transmitted, in any form by any means, electronic, mechanical, photo-copying, recording or otherwise, without the prior permission of the author.

ISBN 0-919692-00-1

Published by Dean Walker's Yorkminster Publishing, Toronto   Printed in Canada

CONTENTS

	AN INTRODUCTION	1
Chapter 1	ONE MAN'S CHILDHOOD	7
Chapter 2	HIS TEENAGE YEARS	15
Chapter 3	FIRST EARNINGS	23
Chapter 4	GETTING INTO BUSINESS	31
Chapter 5	DISCOVERING CANADA	41
Chapter 6	YEARS OF CONSOLIDATION	53
Chapter 7	SPEAKING OF FAMILIES	63
Chapter 8	POLITICAL CAREER	73
Chapter 9	DOING GOOD WORKS	83
Chapter 10	CONTRACT CLEANING	93
Chapter 11	INTRODUCING LAFORTUNE	101
Chapter 12	THE LORD ELGIN	109
Chapter 13	MORE TIME IN HOTELS	117
Chapter 14	NEW U.S. ENTERPRISE	125
Chapter 15	FRIENDS AT THE TOP	131
Chapter 16	DRINKING DAYS	139
Chapter 17	SECRETS OF SUCCESS	147
Chapter 18	CAPITALISTS' MISTAKES	155
Chapter 19	LESSONS OF LIFE	163

NET WORTH was designed and illustrated by Adriaan Aarden of Toronto.

AN INTRODUCTION

This is Chester Everett Pickering

One evening in his second half-century, Chester Pickering stared down from the window of the presidential suite in the Commodore Hotel in New York. He gazed at a dock on the East River flowing darkly below; and simultaneously he stared back through time to when he was thirteen and living as a beggar. One wet night in 1894, cold, coatless, hungry, he had arrived at that very dock. All day he had trudged the streets of the city without eating. Through the evening drizzle he saw a scow laden with junk and covered by a tarpaulin. The lonely boy crawled between the hard layers of the tarp and, warm and dry at last, slept.

That was the scene that Chester Everett Pickering, O.B.E., industrialist, millionaire, remembered in 1950 as he relaxed, drink in hand, in the finest suite of a luxury hotel owned by his friend William Zeckendorf. He found himself musing: "It's not all *that* far from down there to up here." This book is, in part, the story of that journey.

In 1973, C.E. Pickering is ninety-two years old, with clear eyes, a straight back, and enough energy to outpace many men twenty-five years younger. He's chairman of the board of Dustbane Enterprises Limited, the Canadian company that grossed $32-million in 1971; and of Michael's Industrial Equipment Limited that recently launched a United States enterprise that may outgrow Dustbane. He controls Ottawa's Lord Elgin Hotel and came close to owning Toronto's Lord Simcoe as well. He has been an alderman and a controller in Ottawa and has worked and played and fought and laughed with the poor and the rich, the famous and the unknown.

He has five daughters, fourteen grandchildren, 28 great grandchildren, two great great grandchildren, and he and his third wife are about to celebrate their fiftieth wedding anniversary. He spends his winters in Florida where he heads for the racetrack six afternoons a week; and his summers in Ontario and Quebec where he fishes, and spends more time at the track.

He is alert, imaginative, ambitious, and — surprising for his years — quite tolerant. Despite the rough experiences of his early teens, he feels life has treated him well and finds that, even now, apart from the loss of irreplaceable friends, every year is somehow richer, warmer than the one before. In 1973 he has time to think about life and its subtleties and now knows that, even at ninety-two, a man can't come close to solving the basic mysteries of life. He says: "The predominant question every day is still: *why?*"

"Why are men, and that includes Chester E. Pickering, so *stupid?* Why do they cheat each other? Why can't they go to work and sort things out and make them better? All they need to do is use their God-given intelligence." Simple questions, they prove as unanswerable at ninety as at nineteen.

Chester Pickering's own journey through the big and small question marks of life is the classic North American trip: from the bottom to the top in a lifetime. He has exploited the opportunities of free enterprise competitive capitalism; he's grateful to the system for what it has let him achieve and wants capitalism to survive; but he is worried about it. He is alarmed at the *short-sightedness* of many of his fellow industrialists. He thinks the *greed* and entrenched power of so many of them threatens the very system they are prospering under. Capitalism, he suspects, cannot survive without modification and if inflexible, intolerant, unimaginative men stand in the way of such modifications the whole structure may topple. "We may be living in a fool's paradise," he warns. "Remember — the French and Russian ruling classes felt secure before the revolution. They ignored the danger signs that surrounded them. It's important that we get the people at the top in free enterprise to start *thinking.*" His earthy background protects him from the dogmatism that paralyzes the thinking of many men of age and wealth. Even as he sounds his warning, he insists: "I'm just asking people to *think* about these things." Private enterprise is on trial; powerful forces are out to destroy it; in just fifty-five years communism has blanketed a large area of the world. He agreed to talk about his experiences and ideas as a contribution to this debate.

Introduction 3

For Pickering, no ideas — from Christian Science to Social Credit — can be dismissed without study. He remembers back to the early years of this century when the very idea of socialism was considered lunacy. One fall when he employed casual labor to pick apples in an orchard, someone mentioned that his gang included a man who was running as *socialist* candidate for Governor of Rhode Island. "I went down and looked at him. He didn't *look* crazy!" Nor do socialist ideas seem "crazy" to Pickering. He prefers capitalism — but not the capitalism of the blind. There's room for modification.

In the middle of his life he dived with enthusiasm into politics, campaigning on the strength of his success as a businessman. His appointment to an arbitration board at the time was labeled unfair because his fellow employers considered him "a friend of labor". The charge delighted him. In a later speech he responded: "We always hear of racketeers in labor groups but we never hear of the racketeers in the capitalist class. Racketeers are bad for both classes. We must all be sure we get rid of the people who sponge on us."

When an old man looks back he can't avoid some rewriting of history, some rationalization. Pickering claims, for example, that he always tried to avoid the spotlight, yet public life attracted him hypnotically. He is still bewildered that people wouldn't accept at face value his election statements that his only motivation was "a keen desire to use my ability for the good of the community". Similarly about business: he likes to recall his "total honesty", spends less time recalling and analyzing his equal dedication to winning every business battle.

Nevertheless he is more objective than most. He doesn't recall his actions entirely through rose-colored rationalizers. He can acknowledge that he was impatient with people who couldn't think or move fast enough; that he was prickly to deal with; that he manipulated others. "I wish I'd softened sooner," he says. He knows he is no saint. He is also aware that neither saints nor supermen exist, so he'll waste no time wearing a hairshirt for the mistakes he made.

Today he lives comfortably, modestly, quietly. Recently he bought his first racehorses and this adds zest to those days without number he spends at the track. Typical of Pickering, the horses do more winning than losing, and in his very first year he showed a profit. "If I can get my Horseman's Badge and ponce around with those fancy people, and just break even, that's all I want to achieve." As he says that, you need to watch his eyes, because he's kidding you; he has no interest at all in "fancy people". In food, friends, lifestyle, he enjoys the real, the unpretentious, not the fancy.

Life is good at ninety-two and he is glad he has lived so long. There were two times, however, when he almost decided not to bother. There was the month when his second wife died and, a half-century later, he can still weep quietly at the memory of the pain he felt then. He thought it not worth the effort of carrying on, until he realized his Stella would have wanted him to.

Thirty years later, in his mid-seventies, he again contemplated quitting. With his children and his companies well-established and his obligations met, he thought he might just as well coast downhill the rest of the way with a good book and a glass of good brandy. Then a friend said: "You're hurting the people around you." He called again on his unusual capacity for being objective, put down the glass, and went back to work. Since then he has not had a drink and has already added twenty more constructive years to his life.

So far, then, it has been a rewarding life. He's given and taken, and he's learned. And one Friday morning recently, at the urging of his family and many friends, Chester E. Pickering sat back in an armchair, blinked those very clear eyes at me a couple of times as he gazed back into his past, and we began to talk about it. . . .

Dean Walker
October, 1973
Toronto, Canada.

Chapter 1

ONE MAN'S CHILDHOOD
Unlikely source of strengths

Mr. Pickering, you see the world from a special viewpoint: through the binoculars of age and financial success. You've lived through periods that most of us can only know from history books, and your success is obvious in the status of the companies you have launched.

When you were born, in Massachusetts in 1881, it was a most paradoxical time. In that period following the Civil War, when the United States had only a quarter of the people and a seventy-fifth of the Gross National Product that it has today, it somehow offered more job opportunities than had ever before been available anywhere. Technology and optimism were soaring in mutual support as new marvels — electricity, the telephone, the elevator — changed daily life. Technology was also luring Americans into the perpetual motion that later characterized them. Railroads had closed the distance between the coasts to a mere seven days and when Nellie Bly, girl reporter, circled the world in seventy-three days, she symbolized a quick new spirit.

And yet those last thirty years of the nineteenth century also saw three major depressions. During the worst of them, in 1893, a survey revealed the existence of 46,000 tramps. In that land of overflowing job offers, these tens of thousands of men, nearly all able to read and equipped with adequate work skills, had deliberately "dropped out" of the conventional world to live without fixed address and employment, and by their own behavior code.

Children often dropped out too. Although school attendance was compulsory in thirty-one states (and had been for two centuries in Massachusetts), that didn't mean much. Schools of that day were later described as "robot parade-grounds for the mind", and every lesson was taught by rote. When any lad, fed up with such a deadening approach, decided to play Tom Sawyer for a while, there was no way to bring him back until he himself decided to show up and take his caning. If he ran away permanently, the underdeveloped communications and law enforcement systems left him free to roam as he pleased.

Family life was sentimentalized. As one observer has noted wryly: "Men with hard hands and moist eyes sang *Home Sweet Home* as they bellied up to the bar." When an itinerant photographer with his horsedrawn darkroom came by, the whole family posed for a solemn record of togetherness to be preserved in the family album or hung with pride on the parlor wall. Yet in the family, too, hints of coming change could be found. Women were less willing to be subservient, and between 1870 and 1900 annual divorce totals increased from eleven thousand to 56,000. By 1890, nearly four million women had joined the labor force.

Communities of the day were smaller and more closely knit. Relatives and neighbors looked out for each other, and insurance for those who fell ill comprised home-baked pies or beans or soup from concerned friends, or firewood stacked anonymously at the kitchen door. Church and school were centers of community life; recreation, such as a barn dance after a barn-raising bee, was usually in celebration of a good job done.

In the industrialized states, however, more people now spent their time working for wages, mostly in factories. Clothing factories, expanded during the Civil War, converted easily to mass production and by the 1890s employed one-and-a-half-million people. Seven out of ten industrial workers earned as little as ten cents an hour. Often the workers were children, some only three years old, tackling simple tasks such as making paper collars. Two million children under fifteen — one in five — were earning maybe twenty-five cents for the normal ten-to-twelve hour day. "The factories need the children and the children need the factories," declared the industrialists piously. By modern standards, working conditions were appalling.

Of course life was not all gloom and sweat. Annual income *was* climbing: from $779 to $1,164 in those thirty years. The average work day gradually decreased from twelve to ten hours. Thus many had the time and money to seek out entertainment. They turned to the traveling circuses on horsedrawn wagons, to trolley rides and comic books and the earliest moving pictures. Vaudeville, burlesque, minstrel shows, and plays, P.T. Barnum and Buffalo Bill, and New York's first baseball team all competed for audiences. Light, noisy, fast-moving plays, lurid melodramas, lively variety shows were theatre favorites.

Four million Americans rode bicycles. Libraries segrated books by women from books by men. New York had twenty-storey skyscrapers. Hydraulic elevators climbed at six hundred feet per minute. That was the world you were born into, Mr. Pickering, and it was indeed a long time ago. Since then Hollywood and wishful thinking have sentimentalized the 1880s as idyllic, less worldly times, when all marriages were made in Heaven and every child's homelife rested on a stable Victorian rock. Were your childhood and homelife idyllic?

MY CHILDHOOD! It was far from idyllic. We lived in East Blackstone, Massachusetts, but never really had a home, because my father and mother didn't get along. During the first seven years of my life they kept separating and then finally parted for ever. Even while they were "together", we lived at my grandparents' or at somebody else's house. So I really had no home.

I don't have unhappy memories although I sometimes wonder what it would have been like to have had more real "childhood". I loved my parents, I think, although I can remember even then being determined that I would amount to more than my father did when I grew up.

I have an almost photographic memory of the earliest years. I can "see" my father's mother's funeral which happened when I was less than three years old. I was taken to my grandparents' house and someone said: "Take the baby upstairs. There's a girl there to look after him." The *baby!* I was highly insulted. Right now I can *see* the woman who said that. I can still *feel* my three-year-old resentment.

East Blackstone had a dozen or so houses and that neighborhood virtually adopted me. Time and again when things were going badly between my parents, the neighbors would take me in and feed me, or give me a place to sleep. Everybody was my father, everybody my mother, every house my home. I could turn up anywhere at mealtimes and be fed. Half the time my mother and father couldn't have known where I was.

I was always headstrong. On many days, instead of going to school, I roamed the woods. I'd get a line and a hook and fish all day; it was the life of Riley! Skipping school was fairly common then, and the teachers didn't punish me for it. Sometimes my mother followed me to school to make sure

I got there, walking about fifteen yards behind me. If I sat down on a rock hoping she'd get tired and go away, she'd just wait me out. On those days I'd eventually get up and go along to school.

When things made no sense to me at the one-room schoolhouse, I refused to pay attention. Spelling, for example, made no sense at all; nor did grammar. I couldn't see how either mattered very much as long as people could understand what I wrote. Even today I spell words the way they sound.

I never needed to *learn* much arithmetic. I went no further than decimal fractions, yet I've always been able to get mathematical answers in my head. The other day my son-in-law and I were working on a business problem involving percentages. He was starting to use one of those little pocket computers to figure something out when I gave him the answer. He put down his gadget and grumbled at me: "What's the use of fooling with this thing?"

But getting back to my childhood. . . .

My father was a happy-go-lucky fellow who never took life seriously. He was more interested in having people *like* him than in achieving anything else. At least he was successful in that: he was very popular. My mother was exactly his opposite. She was of French descent and very fiery, very highly-strung. Her people were all industrious mill-workers and she fought to make my father that type of man. There was no way. Dad would be into one thing today and something else tomorrow. He could do anything; he was a painter, a paperhanger, a carpenter, a farmer, he could fix shoes or boots. But he never settled. Once he invented a product to make us all rich: pumpkin ketchup! It looked and tasted OK and local stores even stocked and sold it. Until the bottles started exploding. He didn't know much about preservatives.

He was *kind* enough; he took me to circuses. But he would get my mother mad by laughing and joking with all the pretty girls in the village. Probably he was never actually out of line with a girl, but there was always someone ready to start trouble by telling stories to my mother. When she criticized him, however, he never fought back; he just laughed which exasperated her still more and she'd pack and move back to her mother's house. Dad would stick that out for a week, then he'd go over and promise her the world and get her back again. Then she'd leave again. We children — I had two younger brothers — couldn't understand it.

When my parents separated permanently, I stayed in the neighborhood with my father. One brother went with my mother and the other was adopted and brought up under a different name in a lovely home and given a fine education. Oddly enough both brothers became tool-makers; they inherited my father's skills with his hands. I didn't. I can't drive a nail.

I adored my grandparents who were totally kind-hearted. After grandmother died, my grandfather lived alone and, as he had to leave for work at about half-past-five each morning, he couldn't do much cooking, so he brought home bread and pies and doughnuts from the bake shop. A couple of friends and I always went into grandfather's house and gorged ourselves on his leftover pies and doughnuts.

He was a very cross-looking man. When he glared at you over his glasses, you'd run and hide yet, scared as we were, we stole his bakestuff for years. It was only later that I realized the game he was playing; he bought much more than he needed in order to feed us three kids. He made it seem as if we were stealing because we'd have no fun if he hadn't. He was one of the kindest men I ever met. He lived to be ninety-one. Not a bad age.

The water power of the Blackstone River attracted textile mills that were terrible sweatshops. Immigrants from Europe who worked there would be dying of tuberculosis within two or three years. When the New England authorities finally clamped down, the textile companies simply moved their mills to the southern states to exploit black labor instead.

It was horrible for poor people in those days, probably worse than Southern slavery had been. If they could get a few acres of land to grow food and cut firewood, they got along fairly well, but those who had to be employed were treated worse than slaves. People worked in those mills, twelve hours a day, six days a week. They bought their supplies at a store owned by the company, and lived in a company house. At the end of each week they owed the company more than the whole family had been able to earn, even though the wife and the father both worked, and so did children from seven years old.

When I was about ten I talked my father into getting me a job in one of those mills, so I could have a few dollars of my own. My job was to splice the yarn when it broke but I was hopeless at it; by the end of each day I'd have all the colors mixed up. I hated the place, but there was to be one compensation: I waited desperately for that first Saturday night when I would see a tangible return for my work.

As everyone was paid I shuffled along in line towards the desk but, when it came to my turn, the man said: "There's nothing for you. Your father collected your wages." The money was already on its way into a till in some tavern. I quit on the spot.

My father married again when I was about eleven and his new wife was only five years older than me. In a very short time she and I were in conflict in an unspoken but bitter contest for my father's affections. Having us in the same house was like trying to mix oil and water. Just the sight of me aggravated her. The breaking point came when I was thirteen. I got out of bed one morning and slumped into the kitchen where she had just finished cooking oatmeal. As I came through the door she had poured it into a dish ready to serve. She and I stared at each other sullenly for a minute until, without a word, she threw the dish of oatmeal at my head.

It hit the door above me and boiling porridge splattered over my face. I grabbed for a towel to wipe it off, but she got there first and used the towel to swipe me over the head instead. I seized her wrists, backed her against the wall and . . . my father walked in.

I forget what he said but he quickly settled the fight. Then I left. I ran away from home.

Chapter 2

HIS TEENAGE YEARS
Seeing society from the bottom

You didn't exaggerate; your childhood *was* far from idyllic. Nevertheless, running away can't have been easy. That was the year of the Panic of '93, which was a sizeable economic depression. Things were so tough that year that people from all over the U.S. set out to march on Washington, following the guidance of Jacob Coxey, a social reformer. "Coxey's army" was expected to hit Washington on May Day 1893 with 100,000 men. Crowds cheered them on in the cities as they passed through, tramping or riding the rods. By the time they reached the Capitol, however, there were only five hundred left, and Coxey and the other leaders were arrested for walking on the lawn. Jack London was one of those marchers and he describes life among the wandering poor of 1893 in some of his books.

So it was quite a year that you picked to take to the roads. However I don't suppose that, at the age of thirteen, you were worrying much about a Depression. What did you think you were going to do? Weren't you scared? Didn't your father come looking for you? And what about the police? Wouldn't they send home any stray boy they saw wandering around?

DAD DIDN'T BOTHER. He didn't try to find me, because he knew he could do nothing with me. I was too strong, and too headstrong. I went back once, some years later, but didn't stay long. After my father died, however, my stepmother and I met again and became the closest of friends. (Sometimes she said she had married the wrong one of us!) I learned that she was a wonderful woman and we hit it off famously until she died.

His teenage years

The police picked me up once, at about one o'clock in the morning in some city in Connecticut, and questioned me very carefully. I gave them some story that I was on my way home. I was a good talker and they let me go.

I just walked away from that house in East Blackstone, left no note, had no money, no real plan, except for the idea of going to Worcester, near Boston, where my mother lived. It wasn't that I especially wanted to see her but, a week earlier, a circus had visited Blackstone on its way to Worcester and I liked the sound of "running away to join the circus". Whatever that meant.

The only transportation in those days was by train, by horse and buggy, or by foot. Forty miles seemed too far to walk so I pulled a trick I'd often seen the unemployed do; I sneaked onto a freight car. And, after a while, the train rumbled away down the line, away from my "home", into the world.

Freight trains rarely went far without stopping and it took all day for this one to get anywhere near Worcester. When it stopped on a sidetrack, I climbed down.

Coxey's "army of the unemployed" involved men who wanted to work and were angry that there was no work for them to do. But there were also in those days hundreds of full-time tramps who were determined they *never* would work, and made a business of begging. As I climbed down from my freight car on that siding I saw one of these tramps jump off another. I couldn't think what else to do so I followed him as he walked along a little path into the bush.

He led me into a jungle camp, one of the places where bums regularly congregated and loafed around together for a few days. They all knew where to meet, and every evening drifted in to such places two or three at a time. Usually there'd be a big pot of food cooking and each man threw something into it.

As we walked into this camp, the fellow I was following turned and asked me where the hell I thought I was going. I told him some story and he seemed to take a fancy to me; he didn't send me away.

I was now in a strange fraternity of very tough-seeming guys, but this one man I had attached myself to was very kind and I stayed close to him. I slept amongst them that night and next day left when my "friend" left. He was about twenty-five years old and I stayed near him for some weeks. I think he worried that he might get into trouble traveling with such a young runaway boy and sometimes he'd try to sneak off when I wasn't looking, but I wouldn't let him get away.

The gang of bums moved slowly because they loafed around a lot. I don't think they stole things or broke the law much; they just didn't want to work. To eat, they "bummed" food and, after a while, they found I could be an asset to them, because I could accomplish things that they couldn't. When I begged for food I always got more than I needed, and brought back extra with me.

It's a peculiar thing. Even as young as that, I was able to figure out a better way to achieve what I was after. I wasn't prepared to be just a beggar; I would be a better beggar. I didn't "beg" at all. I knocked on doors then said to the lady of the house: "Could you give me some wood to cut? I need something to eat and I'd like to do some work to earn it." They'd always say: "Oh you poor boy. You come on in here." When they asked me why I was begging and where I was going, I'd pretend I was heading for some specific place or was on my way home. Then I'd sit down at the table to a banquet and when I left they always handed me a bag of stuff. I'd take that back to my friends in the jungle. And, really, I lived well. It's amazing how many kind people there are in this world. Those women gave me the best.

The tramps kept me with them as they drifted slowly toward Camden, New Jersey, a languid journey of six or seven weeks. En route, we had to pass through New York where hobos — ten or fifteen in every train that pulled in — always unloaded before daylight at the freightyards in the north-east section of Harlem.

Our gang was heading towards a mission in Jersey City where a man without money could chop wood to earn a meal and a night in a warm bed. That's how it was that, one morning, I found myself alone at the end of Third Avenue knowing only that the East River and Brooklyn Bridge and the ferries to the mission were somewhere down at the other end. I had no money and I knew I couldn't beg food from shops and offices; but in all the places I'd been I'd never known any street I couldn't walk in an hour, so I set off.

That street in New York took me *all day* to walk. Of course, as any boy would, I stopped and marveled at the people and horses and the first elevated train I'd ever seen. But the fascination wore off as the day wore on and, on an empty stomach, I plodded on endlessly on that hard pavement. Third Avenue seemed at least thirty miles long.

18   His teenage years

I remember stopping once to just stare and stare at a three-cent bun in a bakery window. I could just imagine what it would taste like . . . in my mouth . . . chewed slowly. . . . Even today, eighty years later, I can still remember what I thought it would taste like.

For the last hour of that walk, the rain drifted and drizzled and I had no coat so I was both hungry and soaked and felt I was walking on my knees. Moored in the river when I reached it was a scow carrying a pile of junk covered by a tarpaulin. There was no one around so I crawled in under that canvas. I was snug and dry and felt safe hidden in there out of the rain and slipped into the best night's sleep of my life.

Next morning the sun was shining again. I found some brownstone houses where I was able to beg some food. On a full stomach after a fine night's sleep, I felt almost cheerful as I wandered down to the ferries.

The bums had taught me some tricks, and one was how to ride New York ferries when you have no money; you tell a policeman at the docks that you live in New Jersey and are stranded. To get you off his beat and off his mind, the policeman will order the ferry people to let you aboard. On this sunny morning I pulled that trick, and it worked. After a pleasant ride in the ferry I walked to the Jersey City mission and found my wandering friends.

We all chopped our wood dutifully and spent the night at the mission. Next day, we drifted on to Camden, and from there walked across the railroad bridge to Frankfurt, Pennsylvania.

As we reached the other side, however, railroad police, dressed in civilian clothes and armed with long night sticks, appeared from nowhere and arrested us all for trespassing. There was no fight in any of us and they easily loaded us all into a boxcar. This police squad then spent the whole day picking up groups of tramps. They planned to send us to appear before a judge in Philadelphia. When the train started, twenty or twenty-five of us were locked in there in the dark. I was terrified.

They weren't very smart policemen; they had let one of the men keep his big knife. This fellow immediately started to whittle a hole to lever open the boards at the end of the boxcar. It took him an hour or more as we rumbled through the dark getting closer and closer to that judge who I was sure was going to lock me in jail and throw away the key. Finally he weakened the joint enough, and another husky man hauled himself up on a crosspiece and kicked out a couple of slats. As I was the smallest I was the first one out. For a minute I stood on the coupling between the swaying cars, then jumped out into the dark.

I tumbled down and down and down an embankment but somehow did myself no real harm. By the time I had got on to my feet, the train had disappeared. I was completely on my own.

I turned and walked away from the railroad. There would be no more freight cars for me; I never rode another train illegally in my life. Nor did I ever see those men again.

On the way through Jersey City the people at the mission had urged me to go back to my home. This I would never do. But now, scratched and bruised in the dark, I knew I didn't want to be alone any more and wondered if that mission couple might be kind to me. I headed back to Jersey City.

I walked along country roads all the way, about ninety miles. En route I asked farmers if they would give me a job, but none of them would. I begged them to hire me, said I'd work for *nothing,* but nobody was interested in taking me. I'd never been so alone in my life, and swore I never would be again.

One night I crawled into a shed and lay down on a pile of steel rails. Then another tramp climbed in. He seemed friendly enough and I fell back to sleep. I have heard since that brutal homosexuality was common in the hobo jungle, but the bums I had traveled with had been decent and kind to me. In the middle of this night, however, I awoke with this man mauling at me. In the pitch dark we fought like tigers. I was desperately frightened and, although only thirteen, was very strong. We fought and cursed and cried on that pile of iron in the dark and I hit him and hit him with my fist because in the dark I couldn't find anything else to hit him with. Somehow, finally, I subdued him and escaped. I just left him lying there. Maybe I killed him, I don't know. I almost hope that I did. I *could* have killed him I was so frightened.

I finally limped back into Jersey City and the people at the mission insisted that I stay. "You have no home. Stay here while we try to locate your parents." That was going to be difficult for them, because I had told them my name was Bebeau — my mother's maiden name — and I wouldn't tell them where I came from.

I stayed at that mission for nine months, eating meals with the ministers, choosing clothes from all the second-hand stuff that people gave to the mission, attending compulsory church service every evening, sleeping in the dormitory with the tramps.

I handled a number of regular jobs for them such as taking charge of the wood-sawing operation. And the mission had an arrangement with a high-class restaurant to take all its left-over food, so every morning I'd enlist a tramp from the dormitory and we'd load a big basket at the restaurant's back door. My temporary assistant and I then always stopped in an alley and gorged ourselves on the best of the pickings, before taking the rest back to the mission. Another daily job was taking a push-cart down to the Hudson River to meet the boat that ferried in the ice. There were no refrigerators in those days so ice was cut by handsaw out of northern lakes and shipped south insulated in sawdust.

The tramp from whom I inherited this daily job explained something to me very carefully. "The mission people always give you a dime to buy a block of ice," he said. "But you *never* buy a ten-cent block! Always buy a nickel piece, and keep the other five cents for beer."

"But they'll know it's only a five-cent block!"

"No they won't," he said triumphantly. "In all these years, they've never *seen* a ten-cent block!" Thus for the nine months I stayed in Jersey City, my daily routine included a short stop at a saloon where a nickel bought two big glasses of beer.

I finally left the mission because I wanted to get on with my life and thirty or forty years later when I drove back there again, the mission was torn down and nobody knew what had become of the people. For the life of me I can't remember that couple's name.

I wouldn't have missed that year I lived as a tramp for anything in the world. I've always been glad that I had the chance to know those lonely tough pathetic hobos, and to experience their strange and desolate world. I learned a lot in those months about how cold — and how warm — the world can be. Perhaps that's why today I can't be bothered living in any fancy way and why I'm more at home with real people, not with those who think a million dollars is something worth degrading yourself for. It was the real people, not the rich, who were kind to me when I was a kid wandering around.

st Blackstone School, 1885

Chapter 3

FIRST EARNINGS

He learns he has drive, ambition

You wanted to "get on with your life" because even then, at fourteen, you knew you wanted to be somebody. Yet surely the odds were heavily against you. You had no education, no family, no understanding of the world. And that wasn't today's affluent world where basic needs are almost guaranteed: even by 1900 the average wage was only twelve dollars for a sixty-hour week.

Has it occurred to you in looking back that you were trying to live the classic American Dream? As one biography of Horatio Alger Jr. points out, "The moguls of the last century were almost entirely poor boys who began at the absolute bottom of the ladder" and most of them had "only a perfunctory education". That certainly describes you. Alger met many homeless urchins such as you and, because most made their living as newsboys, he concocted his famous melodramatic newsboy-to-president stories from their dreams.

You didn't sell newspapers, but you did become president of a number of companies. How did you ever get started?

HELP WAS NEEDED. And the only person I could think of who might be helpful to me when I left the mission was my father's brother, Ralph, a blacksmith in Windsor, Connecticut.

In those days a blacksmith was the aristocrat of workers. He could earn three times as much as most other men, and Uncle Ralph gave me a very fair break. For nine months he let me live with his family while he tried to teach me his trade; but I remained as hopeless as ever with my hands. Finally one night my dumb mistakes got him so exasperated that he took me by the collar and the seat of the pants and threw me out of his shop. "You won't make a blacksmith," he shouted at me, "if you try for a million years!" I had to admit he was right. He bought me a ticket on the steamcar to Blackstone and sent me back to my father.

My father and stepmother by now had two new children (they eventually produced eleven) and I suppose she was too busy to let my presence in the house bother her so much. I spent a winter working in the woods with my father, chopping wood at a dollar a cord. But I soon grew restless. When the spring came I left again, this time to visit my mother in Worcester. She was now a housekeeper to Joe Santam, a well-established contractor, and had calmed down a lot. Her French temper didn't flare so often.

Santam kept teams of horses for ploughing, hauling wood and stone, or handling any other suitable work and he gave me a job at eight dollars a month. As he could neither read nor write, it became my job to read the newspaper to him; and he couldn't keep books, so I made notes about all his jobs and the people he worked for. For four years I was his reader, secretary, and hired man.

One of his regular contracts was to bring firewood from eight miles outside Worcester. The roads were unpaved and, when it rained, there were huge instant mudholes. It was on the firewood job that I discovered something about myself: I have total pigheaded determination. On wet muddy days the other drivers, their wagons stuck in the mud, would often give up on the effort to bring back the wood: I never did. Not once. I ferried the load through the mud patches a bit at a time. Sometimes I didn't get it all home until midnight, but I *always* brought the load back. And I learned that, when you're not prepared to quit, you always somehow find a way. Stubborness was born in me and I've been glad of it.

All the drivers who worked for Santam lived with him, and their world became mine. At fifteen, I did a man's work, associated with men, drank like a man.

At some time during that period, for the first time in my life, I tried to *sell* something. A man who was producing horseradish gave me a bucket of it and a wooden scoop and said, if I brought back the empty bucket and four dollars, I could keep a quarter for myself. When I knocked on the first door I was tongue-tied with fright, and the housewife who appeared could not understand English. Finally, to see what I was selling, she popped a spoonful into her mouth and swallowed. Her agonized shriek brought her husband running. There was I standing and stuttering with my bucket of horseradish and his wife turning all shades of the rainbow. That ended my selling career for a while.

One day Joe Santam mentioned that his cousin, a Mr. Newell, needed a hired man for his farm. On the spur of the moment I took the job. For about three years I stayed with the Newells and, for the first time in my life, knew the pleasures of living in a real home. Until then, I had never *dreamed* that such a peaceful, settled homelife could exist.

The style of working I had developed under Santam stayed with me. Whenever I did a job, I had to do it better than anyone else around. If I was haying, I had to get in more hay than anybody else. If I was ploughing, I had to plough more land. I had to *excell*. Maybe I was a boy trying to prove myself a man. Of course Newell — a nice man with a nice wife — thought that was just fine, and I might have stayed there for ever if it hadn't been for the third member of his household.

As well as having a very fine farm and a very fine wife, Newell also had a very fine daughter. She was a few months older than me but I tacked a year on to my age. Like any teen-aged girl, Florence Newell liked parties and dances. She had no brothers or sisters to take her, and her parents were too old, so her father often lent me his horse, his buggy, and his Florence; and it wasn't very long before we had a problem. We became fond of each other and she wanted to marry me.

The Newells, however, didn't want their daughter marrying any hired hand. She was a high school graduate, prominent in her church, an aristocrat for her times. What's more the Newells were vehemently opposed to alcohol and somehow they knew about my father's happy carousing. They were worried I would follow in his footsteps. They made it quite clear to me I wasn't wanted in their family. Although Florence was willing to marry me anyway, I wasn't butting in on any family that didn't want me. I left.

A half-century later, I was near Worcester and went looking for Florence. I found her house and, when she came to the door, she looked at me for a long, long time. Then she cried: "You're Everett!"

She had married a printer and raised two children, and had happy years, but now she was a widow. We quickly became friends again.

A few years after *that,* I was down there again, this time with my wife and daughter and a grand-daughter. I asked them: "Would you like to meet an old sweetheart?" We found Florence, then all took a drive together around our old haunts. She and I sat in the front seat, reminiscing, rediscovering places, driving over the old roads we used to travel on our bicycles, peering back through sixty years. My wife and daughter and grand-daughter sat in the back hearing and enjoying it all. In those three generations of younger women enjoying our pleasure, there was just no meanness.

Florence Newell is still alive and every now and again I send her oranges from Florida. Good Heavens: she's ninety-four!

When I left the Newells, I returned to my mother who was now living in an apartment in Worcester. I found a job with a landscape gardener there and enjoyed it well enough, but I was always hankering to work with horses. The summit of my ambition was to drive the smartest team with the shiniest harness.

A man called Gleason, owner of a Worcester produce company, had teams with exceptionally shiny harnesses. I landed a temporary job doing seasonal work in his warehouse, but my real aim was to drive for him when his regular season started in the spring. I worked out a plan to become noticeable.

All the other temporary workers just wanted to get in and get out and get paid, but I arranged my schedule so that, when Mr. Gleason arrived for work at six each morning, he always had to step over me to unlock the door. I *always* arrived before everybody else. And when he left each evening, I was always the last person he saw. At the end of the season, I asked him if he would take me on as a teamster when his business moved again in March. He said without hesitating: "You're hired right now for the spring. Come on March 16th." Three days later I received a postcard from him: "Report tomorrow." He had created a job for me shoveling potatoes into box cars.

One day during that winter, he suddenly said: "Get on a bicycle and go down to Joe Beardsley's store and replevin our stuff." I had no idea what "replevin" meant, but I didn't want to admit that.

Beardsley had gone bankrupt and I found the sheriff waiting at his store. He said gruffly: "You can reclaim any stuff that's Gleason's. But if you take anything that isn't his, you'll be arrested." I looked at all the produce and wondered how *anyone* could tell what had come from Gleason's and what had come from elsewhere. Eventually I drove back to the warehouse with our wagon heaped with produce. When he saw it, Gleason chuckled with glee, like a man who has lost a dime and found a quarter. The next day he fired one of his junior salesmen and gave me the poor fellow's job at nine dollars a week.

I don't know what made Gleason think I could *sell*. I certainly hadn't succeeded the time I tried to sell the horseradish. The first day I went out for Gleason was an incredibly cold Wednesday in December and I didn't sell a thing. At nightfall, totally discouraged, convinced I'd be fired, I dragged my feet back to the warehouse to find Gleason and a friend sitting close to the pot-bellied stove. He looked startled that I had even *tried* to sell on such a cold day. "How did you do?" he asked.

I told him glumly. He stared at me and, for a moment, time stopped. Then he gave me a slap on the back that nearly knocked me into the fire. "Don't worry young fellow," he bellowed. "You'll get paid on Saturday night. Try again tomorrow." Three-quarters of a century later I still look back on that moment as a turning point in my life. If Gleason had discouraged me, I might never again have tried to sell. But he didn't discourage me and I didn't quit; and the next day I went out again and sold something. Within twelve months I was his top salesman and earning a thousand dollars a year. Big money. Now I was the aristocrat. I wish Newell could have seen me.

Gleason's attitude was a break for me. Most successful men's careers are built around breaks of that sort, but few whom I've met will admit it.

*Five generations.
Clockwise from
C.E. Pickering (top right):
His grandfather,
his grandson,
his father,
his daughter*

*C.E. Pickering (seated)
at twenty-one;
his Mother and brothers
Ernest, Arnold (right)*

Chapter 4

GETTING INTO BUSINESS
Green and his green stuff

Your attempt on that first day to sell in the rain reminds me of the story of Joseph P. Day, a famous salesman who was in action about ten years before you. He made a point of selling during the worst weather when other salesmen stayed home. In that way, Day met his customers in an unhurried atmosphere without competitors breathing down his neck, and in that special cosiness you always find inside on a stormy day. He received his first big salary raise when he fought his way through a raging blizzard to win an order.

Penrose Scull tells Day's story in *From Peddlers to Merchant Princes,* a book that spells out the historical significance of salesmanship in North America. He explains that last century the assets of average people here were only their natural talents and skills. They had no rich class to lean on for support. They could only grow or make things, then try to sell them to each other. An American wanting to dispose of a sack of potatoes or a hand-made chair had to use a lot of persuasion to get a neighbor to part with hard cash and this put an emphasis on selling that didn't exist anywhere else. Because economic necessity usually made it urgent to close the sale, hard sell rather than subtlety was the rule.

As there was no large rich class, goods had to be produced in volume to sell at low prices and that approach, too, was quite different from the European tradition. Hundreds of colonists fiddled with contraptions to produce more faster for less and, whenever a man succeeded in doing that,

32 Getting into business

he had a sudden production capacity that usually swamped available distribution facilities. Again he faced a special need to *sell*. Thus the salesman became the North American industrial hero.

So when Gleason gave you the chance to become a "salesman", he made you part of a business development that helped establish the flavor and speed of North America.

How long did you stay with him?

GLEASON TAUGHT ME A LOT. I stayed with him long enough to learn all he knew about produce and buying and selling, and that was a lot. It was Gleason who said to me: "Price and principle both start with a 'p' and the best principle is not to cut prices."

Some customers bicker and dicker over every price, while others are content to pay a fair price as stated. Gleason pointed out that, if you're prepared to cut prices, you'll usually do so for the man who haggles and not for the friendly, decent guy who doesn't. What could be more illogical than giving the better deal to the guy who's unpleasant to deal with! To this day, none of my companies will cut prices. We tell all our customers: "Our price includes a fair profit and we won't go below it." People worth dealing with accept that.

I figured out another business lesson for myself while working for Gleason: when my customers learned that they could *trust* me they were happier buying from me than from someone they couldn't trust. So I worked to earn their trust. I always carefully selected the best produce for them, and I never sent them more than the exact quantity I was sure they could sell.

I was twenty now and wanted to move ahead fast because I had new personal responsibilities: I was married. A divorcee had been living with her young son next door to my mother's apartment. Jenny was older than me, but I developed a protective feeling toward her and married her in 1901, and in the next five years we had three daughters. In an attempt to earn more money to buy food for all these mouths, I left Gleason and went into business on my own. He and I stayed on friendly terms, however, and continued to do business together.

Food and produce was a very seasonal business because there was no proper refrigeration. Oranges froze in the cold weather, bananas rotted when it was hot. Each fall, both Gleason and I had to curtail our activities until spring. Henry Green, who rented my first place of business to me, knew I was a restless go-getter and was always impatient waiting for spring so, in the winter of 1906, he suggested I visit Boston and meet his brother George who had just invented a "sweeping compound".

The Germans had introduced a sweeping compound based on salt at the St. Louis World Fair in 1904. George Green's stuff was based on sawdust which was a lot cheaper. "But what does it do?" I asked. Henry Green took a handful of a green mixture from a barrel and scattered it on the floor, then took a broom and swept it up. I looked at him blankly. "So?"

"That's what it does! You put in on the floor then sweep it up."

Stupid! He had to be crazy to expect people to pay six dollars a barrel for that.

But it wasn't stupid, and seventy years later I have assets to prove it. Green called his compound Dustbane, and today Dustbane Enterprises Limited and its subsidiaries sell well over thirty million dollars worth of goods and services every year. We are still selling Dustbane itself unchanged in formula seventy years later.

In today's world of broadloom and tiled floors, waxes, detergents, vacuum cleaners and electric polishers, a sweeping compound has limited use (which is why Dustbane Enterprises today also manufactures waxes, detergents, vacuum cleaners and electric polishers). But in 1906 all methods of cleaning were primitive. Floors were of rough lumber, and every time you swept them dust rose in a cloud, blew in and out of your lungs and hair, then settled again. The only way you could beat the dust was to throw damp sawdust onto the floor, but that left unsightly splotches until your warehouse or store looked like a place where you feed chickens. And sawdust didn't *clean*.

Green's Dustbane did — and does — clean. It contains oil to absorb dust, a dye for visibility, nitro-benzol to give it a nice smell, and it leaves a little finish or gloss on the floor. I was skeptical in the winter of 1906 but, with a family to feed and no action in the produce business, I agreed to visit Boston and see this fellow with the green stuff.

George Green knew how to handle a young man. Rather than argue the merits of his product he gave me evidence that it could be sold by showing me his books. His "factory" was a barn, containing a barrel with an electric mixer. His management technique was simple: he'd make a load then go out and sell it.

And he certainly could sell it; he showed me repeat orders from very substantial companies. (Later I came to realize that he was one of the best salesmen I ever would meet.) With the cocksureness of a twenty-five year-old who has run his own business, I had no doubts that, if he could sell it, so could I. I accepted his offer of a $2.10 commission on every six-dollar barrel and, in December 1906, set out to call on the grand merchants of Boston. I was as green as grass; as green as Dustbane! My sample case was a cardboard suitcase my mother had bought ten years earlier for ninety-eight cents. It was idiotic to think that I could sell such established businessmen anything. And I couldn't. I was beaten.

Never before had I been challenged like that. Every day was as bad as that first Wednesday when I went out for Gleason. Only that characteristic which I had found in myself while hauling the firewood — the trait that friends call determination and enemies call pig-headedness — stopped me giving up.

Yet I damned near had to: I had a family to feed and no weekly money to draw on, because Green was always short of cash. He spent every penny he took in to buy more barrels and sawdust. He had the classic small business problem: he was cash-poor and full of potential. I was paid only when I sold something, and it became a race between me learning to sell Dustbane and starving to death. I swore to myself in fury and frustration: "I'll make it. No compromise!" Green offered no advice, no suggestions.

I reached the point where I could sell a bit of the stuff. I could get an *order,* but it was always for a $1.75 box, which paid me twenty-five cents in commission. I had the devil's job earning enough quarters to pay for a bed and food, let alone send money back to Worcester for Jenny. I shared a room in a boarding house; that cost a dollar a week. Breakfast of applesauce, two doughnuts, coffee, cost ten cents. Lunch was a big bowl of beef stew, bread and butter, and coffee: fifteen cents. Supper was always a "Number Ten": cornbeef hash with an egg on top, and coffee, ten cents. Thirty-five cents a day for meals, a dollar a week for a bed, and I could barely earn it!

That dull, slogging, period lasted six months. Spring came and I could have gone back to my fruit and produce business and made a better living, but I wasn't going to quit. Green was doing well selling Dustbane; surely I could too. At the end of six months I swallowed my pride and asked him: "What am I doing wrong?" He told me. I made one small change in my approach and the tide turned. I immediately started making sales and money.

Green's "secret" was elementary. When people asked him, "How does it come packed?", he always replied, "By the 250-pound barrel." Then he'd wait. When people asked *me,* I replied: "By the 250-pound barrel, the 125-pound barrel, and the 12½-pound box." Then they ordered the 12½-pound box. They'd try out the new product in a small quantity and get rid of me at the same time. From that day I don't think I ever again mentioned or sold the 12½-pound box. Later I asked Green: "Why didn't you tell me that in the first place?"

"You weren't in a receptive mood. I had to wait until you were ready to listen." He was seventeen years older than me and knew how to handle a young man.

I took my Dustbane samples and went out on the road. In those days a traveling salesman was usually paid fifty dollars a month plus expenses, but Green paid me commission only. There were bad days when I made only six dollars, but I'd often make thirty and, on outstanding days, I could sell twenty-five barrels and earn fifty. Hotels cost two dollars a day for board and three meals.

I traveled by train throughout New England; one of a large fraternity who spent nights in the pounding Pullman cars, wiggling into our clothes in our berths each morning, shaving precariously in the swaying washrooms. At the turn of the century there were about 100,000 of us who lived and worked that way, each spending up to a hundred nights a year in one of the six thousand Pullman cars. One business historian has described the life we all led: "Traveling salesmen worked hard and long under conditions that, by today's standards, would be considered intolerable. At night they were members of a fraternity of lonely men, swapping stories and experiences in drab hotel lobbies or playing penny ante in a sparsely furnished bedroom lighted by a naked bulb in the ceiling. . . ."

The salesmen I talked and traveled with seemed a peculiar and somehow silly breed. They thought it was smart to cheat on their expense accounts and on the time they put in on the job. They weren't smart enough to realize that, to assess their performance, the company added their expenses and salary together anyway and charged it against the business they brought in.

Unambitious fools, they moved into their territories at noon on Monday, sneaked back home on Friday after lunch, then bragged about this in the smoking cars and hotel rooms. They were only cheating themselves.

They sympathized with me for having such an awful line to sell, for working so hard, for being on commission only. I had to *demonstrate*

36 *Getting into business*

Dustbane from store to store, whereas they had regular sample cases and well-known products and were Big Shots! They'd tell me: "Look I'll get you a job with my firm." I pretended to be grateful and never hinted that I often made as much in a day as they made in a month; they'd only have thought me a liar. Later many of these same fellows applied to me for jobs. I didn't hire them.

I had no one to cheat but myself, so I was out on the job as early as I could get every Monday and never left my territory until eleven o'clock on Saturday night. After a while I traveled by automobile, driving a secondhand Peerless at a time when some New England towns had never seen a car. Sometimes a whole village stopped work when I drove in and the schools let the children out to see my car. That car cut my costs by saving my time and it took me into places that were hard to reach by railroad. *Harper's Weekly* later confirmed what I had already learned when it reported: "The salesman in a trim, speedy little car produces an impression that the salesman on foot or in a horsedrawn buggy never could. The automobile shows that the concern is enjoying prosperity. A new domain is forecast for the automobile, a field that is between that of the pleasure car and the motortruck."

The impression I made in my Peerless didn't hurt sales, and by now I'd made a fine art out of selling Dustbane. I used the whirlwind approach. I'd walk into a store, and look around for the owner, then take up his broom, or assemble the portable one I carried with me. He would watch me, wondering what the devil I was up to. Dramatically, I'd throw down some Dustbane and start sweeping. The demonstration usually impressed him.

I was a quick "closer". I asked him immediately if I could send him a barrel on a thirty-day trial; he could send it back if he didn't like it. I'd write out the order, get his signature, and be gone. Only one man ever returned a barrel and many years later I asked him about it. "I said I'd take one just to get rid of you," he grinned. "When it arrived, I didn't even open it, just shipped it back." But the joke was on him. He soon found that everybody else was using the stuff and he had to send a special order to get some.

By now Jenny and the children were living in Dorchester, a suburb of Boston, in a rented three-decker house. But our marriage wasn't working out. In 1915 she divorced me. I wasn't upset. By then I had met and would soon marry Stella, the truest love of my life.

Throughout this period I soared as a salesman and took Green and his company with me. Soon I wasn't satisfied to be a salesman only. I'd been self-employed once and I knew you can't get very far in life working for someone else. I wanted a piece of the action and I knew how to get it. I deliberately refrained from drawing the big commissions I was earning, and took out only enough to live on. At the end of eighteen months Green owed me more than two thousand dollars, a lot of money for those days. One Saturday I went to him and said: "G.W., I want you to incorporate Dustbane for $25,000 and give me a third of the shares."

"You've gone crazy? I'm not going to do that!"

"Then give me the commission money you owe me." We stared at each other for a while, then I said: "I'll give you a week to think it over. You'll have to pay me, or else sell me the shares for the money you owe me."

Of course he couldn't pay me; he ploughed money back into the business just as fast as he got it. I went back out on the road and had another successful week and on the following Saturday came back into the office. "Have you made up your mind?"

"Made up my mind! What choice have you given me? You know damn' well I can't pay you. I have to give you the shares!"

"That's what I figured."

Now I was a partner and adopted a new title: "Vice-president of sales". I increasingly took over operations and planning and Green followed in back of me.

Although Green was a brilliant salesman he wouldn't work consistently. He'd push for a period then he'd stop, and it might be a month before he'd go back at it again. He didn't have my determination. However he was a great balance for me and I was very fond of him. Where would I have been now without him?

Chapter 5

DISCOVERING CANADA

A new land offers new lessons

So there you were, in the first decade of a new and hopeful century, with a third share of a promising little company. Those must have been stimulating days for a man with your imagination because business had recently been forming many of the shapes and techniques on which its twentieth century expansion would be built.

In mid-century, when A.T. Stewart became the first to set firm prices on the dry goods in his store, that radically altered "selling", because fierce haggling was replaced by discussion of the virtues of the product itself. The change appealed to both customers and businessmen and Stewart's became the largest store in the world. R.H. Macy went further. In his stores there was not only a set price but he sold for cash only. This reduced his overheads, and down came his prices. Then John Wanamaker started taking an interest in quality. His label on a garment gave it a ten-day money-back guarantee. Seedy quality was no bargain at any price, asserted Wanamaker. While these three pushed back merchandising frontiers in the U.S., Timothy Eaton took similar steps in Canada. There, too, the moves were welcomed and Eaton built a fortune.

Business was also starting to learn about mass communication. Eaton's catalogue, with its careful copy and illustrations, sold goods in the remotest parts of Canada. Wanamaker purchased the world's first full-page newspaper advertisement.

As these trends shaped, you had your hands on a small company of some potential. How fast were your sales efforts pushing Green and Dustbane ahead? After you'd been a partner for, say, three years, how big was the enterprise?

THIRTY THOUSAND DOLLARS. That was our gross in 1908. The company comprised the two partners, plus two salesmen, and two men in the factory. That was when I persuaded Green and Dustbane to come to Canada.

Curiosity rather than business zeal prompted me. I hadn't seen much of the world. I'd wandered with the hobos around New Jersey, and I'd sold throughout New England, but that was all. I was captivated by the sight, every Saturday morning, of a boat that docked at Boston and sailed again later that day, heading for Saint John, New Brunswick. I talked Green into joining me on a "business trip" there.

The journey took all night and we landed in Saint John on the Sunday morning, registered in a hotel, then went out to look around. We couldn't get over how strange everyone looked. The good people were all heading to church in their striped trousers, morning coats, top hats. We'd never seen anything like *that* in Boston. Customs in the Maritimes change slowly. Years later I realized how freaky Green and I must have looked to *them*. We were dressed in the latest Boston styles, with wide padded shoulders and tight pants and yellow bulldog-toe shoes.

On Monday morning we went out selling and sold like nobody's business. Green took one side of the street and I took the other and we just mowed those people down. They received us with open arms. I began to like Canada.

As we finished working one street, Green said: "I bet you the price of lunch you can't sell Dustbane to that laundry over there." We went over together and I launched my usual irresistible spiel. The owner looked a bit puzzled but heard me out. Then he said: "I just got through telling your friend here: 'Your name may be Green, and your stuff may be green, but I'm not green enough to buy any!' "

"Yes, yes," I said. "I know all that. But he just bet me a lunch I couldn't get you to take any."

"Oh, it's a *bet* is it! In that case I'll just take a small box. And *bon appetit!*"

We worked St. John for five days, then Green went back to Boston to start filling the orders and I took three weeks to work through to Sydney and Halifax then back to Moncton and Saint John. I would move in to a town and sell until I had plenty of orders, then I'd find a suitable dealer to appoint as our local agent. He'd have a head start with the orders I'd already taken but, to get the agency, had to agree to order more than I'd sold.

In Saint John, by the time Green and I were through, we had very large orders so we offered the agency to Emerson & Fisher, a long-established wholesale hardware merchant. These old firms in New Brunswick and Nova Scotia were tough and hard. Fisher was a Scot of about eighty. His son and another young man were meant to be running Emerson & Fisher, but he never let them run *anything;* they were errand boys. I sold young Fisher an enormous quantity of Dustbane at a time when his father was out. I heard later that, when the old man found out, he said: "Don't take delivery!"

The son backtracked fast. "Don't worry," he said. "They probably won't be able to get it into Canada anyway because of the duty. They'll never deliver." The old man growled: "If they do deliver, don't take it."

About three weeks later young Fisher told him: "Father, Dustbane *are* going to deliver. We can't cancel because I signed the order and there'd be a lawsuit."

"If you *don't* cancel it, I'll fire you. I'll disinherit you. You're a stupid fool to buy that junk!"

Young Fisher was really in trouble. However, he had attended university with a lot of the young businessmen of the city so he went to all his friends and asked them, please, to buy some Dustbane just so he wouldn't be disinherited. "I had to put every one of them over a barrel to save my soul with my father." Of course when the old man found that Dustbane would sell, he forgot all about his threat. That firm remains a Dustbane client today.

On that first Maritimes trip I eventually reached Halifax. I sold plenty of product but had not yet lined up a dealer when I worked my way down to the dock. I looked across the bay at the little community of Dartmouth. It was a beautiful October day and I had been working hard so I decided I deserved a trip in the ferry. In Dartmouth, I found three or four commercial buildings but none seemed big enough to be worth selling to. It was obviously a waste of time going near any of them, but one in particular was dirty with cobwebs and dust in the window. I sat down on the curb to wait for the ferry to take me back to Halifax. But just sitting there, doing nothing, facing that especially dirty building, bothered me. My conscience kept nudging: "Why don't you try over there? What can you lose? You're not selling anything sitting here on the curb."

I walked into the place. It was filthy, horrible-looking, full of old furniture. A tall red-headed fellow of about forty asked: "What can I do for you?" Quite reluctantly I launched my spiel. He paid strict attention, then said: "I'll buy a barrel." Then he asked: "Do you sell direct?"

"No we sell through dealers."

"Who's your dealer for Dartmouth?"

"Nobody. This is the first place I've called."

"How can we get the agency?"

"You have to buy a thousand pounds." He said he'd do that. I suppose he thought he'd sell some to the school or the town hall. Then he said: "Who's your agent in Halifax? How much do we have to buy to get the agency over there?"

"A car-load: 36,000 pounds." That was about twelve hundred dollars' worth.

"I'll take that, too."

I didn't know what to make of it as, in this junk shop that probably didn't have fifty dollars to its name, I wrote out an order for more than twelve hundred dollars' worth of Dustbane. How would they pay for it? Why was I tieing up an agency with such a deadbeat outfit! On the ferry all the way back to Halifax, I cursed myself for a fool.

Opposite the ferry dock was a Bank of Nova Scotia. I went in and asked the manager: "This James Simmonds Limited across the bay. Are they any good?"

"Good for how much?"

"Twelve hundred dollars."

"They can walk in here any time they like and get $100,000." They were the biggest wholesale hardware company in the Maritimes and the following year I made my largest sale ever of Dustbane, twelve carloads, to that very firm.

There's a moral here for all businessmen. Don't take anything for granted. Always investigate, and hold your opinion in abeyance.

Back in Boston, Green had hit a snag. When he tried to ship Dustbane to fill those Saint John orders he found we had to pay *duty*. We'd never dreamed of anything like that and had hardly thought of Canada as a foreign country. As no one in Canadian customs had heard of Dustbane, they listed it under "Otherwise Specified", the category which paid the highest duty of all. We couldn't *afford* to ship to Canada.

However there is very little involved in manufacturing our product. All you need is a whisky barrel — and there were plenty of those in the Maritimes — plus a shaft and some spikes and a motor, some sawdust and sand and oil. Within three weeks Dustbane was shipping from its "Saint John factory", established in the basement of a tenement house. With our main operation in Boston and a small ongoing business in Canada, Green looked after manufacturing in both places, and I kept on selling.

In my second sales trip in Canada, I worked west from Saint John, but ran into difficulties. My whirlwind approach which worked fine in the U.S. and the Maritimes flopped in Montreal. In four-and-a-half days in that bicultural city I failed to make one sale. Here were entirely different people; I couldn't fathom them. They seemed determined not to be "pushed around" by any quick-talking smart aleck of a salesman. I went back to my hotel to dream up a new approach.

Next morning I walked along Sherbrooke Street until I noticed a man of about seventy with a fine set of whiskers working in an office above Gales' Shoes Store. I entered and asked if Mr. Gales would spare me a few minutes and was ushered upstairs to the man with the beard. "Yes, young man," he rumbled. "What is it?" I launched my new sales spiel. It's the approach that these days is mostly used by encyclopaedia salesmen, but at that stage it was original.

"We have selected," I said, "a few of the outstanding merchants of Montreal to try this new product and tell us whether we should introduce it to Canada...." I spread some Dustbane and swept it up with my portable broom. Then he swept some.

"Yes," he said finally, and pontifically from behind the beard, "Yes. I think that might well be something that Canadians would appreciate."

"Well, Mr. Gales, I'd like to send you a barrel of it. After thirty days' use, you could give us an even better opinion."

"That seems very fair."

Thus in Montreal and at all points west from then on, *that* was the way I sold Dustbane. "This is new in Canada and I want your opinion of it...." Dustbane remained "new in Canada" for years. The new style, admittedly, affected my output. In the U.S. and the Maritimes I averaged twenty-five calls a day; in the rest of Canada I never did better than fifteen.

In November 1908 I arrived in Ottawa and took a hack from the station to The Windsor Hotel, a second-class place which was all I could afford. On the way there I fell in love with the city.

Ottawa, chosen in 1857 as the seat of Canadian government, is located at the junction of the Ottawa, Rideau, and Gatineau rivers. Its natural surroundings combined with the impressive government buildings gave it a style and flavor that instantly appealed to me. It seemed a more "American" city than those I'd seen lately and in 1896 Prime Minister Wilfrid Laurier had called it "a Washington of the North". Perhaps it was because an American landscape architect, Frederick Todd, had planned many of its driveways and parks. Its population when I first saw it was about 70,000.

I'd been selling so successfully as I worked my way west that Saint John was now too distant as a shipping point. Dustbane is heavy so freight rates are a big factor in its selling price. I convinced Green that we should establish in Ottawa to cut shipping costs as we pushed westward. I always had it in the back of my mind that someday I would come back there to live. We started manufacturing on the top floors of a warehouse on Sussex Street (it's still there, about half-way down on the right-hand side) and this became our headquarters for Canada.

I kept traveling, expanding our dealer network. One morning I arrived in Kingston and, as usual, refrained from booking into a hotel in case I finished my business during the day and could travel on that night. Along Main Street I noted the hotel I would stay in if I decided to stay the night. During the day, however, I finished my work and returned to the railroad station instead, passing the hotel on the way. Out front was a sign which had not been there that morning: "Smallpox. Quarantined". Stuck inside were the traveling salesmen I'd arrived with that morning. While I continued to sell they would be in quarantine for three weeks. I caught the train for Toronto.

It was a cold and miserable night and I fell asleep in the smoking car. Hours later I was awakened by somebody calling: "Pickering! Pickering! Pickering!" I shouted, "That's me," grabbed my bags, and rushed to the door. The brakeman stopped me just before I jumped to the platform. "You don't get off here," he said. "You're going to Toronto."

"But you called my name. You called Pickering!"

"Called you? The hell I did." He looked at me, long-suffering. "This *town* is called Pickering!"

The following year Green and I decided to open up western Canada. For the round trip fare of $45.95, I would establish Dustbane in British Columbia, and see the Seattle world's fair. I never did see the fair. I arrived in Seattle on a Sunday when it was closed and was just too restless to stay. I went straight on to Victoria, ready to start work on Monday. Later we established a small factory in Winnipeg, and sold fifty-five percent of that to Dunbar Hudson, a well-established local businessman who meant to run it as a sideline.

By now Dustbane was doing nicely throughout Canada, New England, and New York State, through this home-made network of dealers whom I had appointed on my ant-like travels. In 1910, I decided we could expand more quickly and less erratically if we tied in with an established national organization.

In Boston, our dealer was the local branch of the huge Johns-Manville company, one of the world's largest manufacturers of building supplies, with branches throughout North America. The company's beginning had been as humble as Dustbane's. C.B. Manville had started an insulation business in Milwaukee in the 1880s, mixing cement in the cellar of his home and selling it by the pail to his neighbors to cover their furnaces. Even earlier, H.W. Johns had started in *his* basement creating roofing material by pouring hot asphalt from a tea kettle onto a sheet of felt, then passing that through a clotheswringer. The two had merged and Thomas Franklyn Manville, son of C.B., now headed up the business.

Tommy Manville was very much the king of that outfit and quite a famous man. At 29 I traveled to New York and, trying to look self-assured, walked boldly into his office on Pine Street. Still very much a green boy, I barged into the center of the high-finance and high-everything district of New York. Manville was one of those men who talk at top speed in a low voice that's hard to understand and won't let anyone else get a word in edgeways, but somehow I got my story across and Manville took on the national Dustbane dealership for two years. That move, more than anything else, put our company on the map. It was an unusual arrangement.

I joined his company as sales manager for Dustbane, but Dustbane paid my salary. From inside his company I managed the marketing of this one product and it cost him nothing. We manufactured only for Johns-Manville which distributed our line coast-to-coast in Canada and the U.S. I had full charge of the merchandising.

Our deal also called for a certain amount of advertising, including a

48   *Discovering Canada*

Dustbane campaign in the *Saturday Evening Post.* For about a year, with Dustbane selling successfully everywhere, Manville kept stalling on this advertising. He didn't say go and he didn't say no, until finally I stormed into his office and issued an ultimatum: "Do this advertising now. It's part of our contract." He looked at me coolly and said: "I've a good mind to cancel that contract anyway."

"Don't let me change your mind."

Manville said to me: "What does your company pay you?"

"Five thousand a year and expenses."

"I'm canceling the contract. But you stay with me and I'll double your salary."

My working world was collapsing around me but I wasn't going to back down. That offer was no insult; $10,000 a year was an enormous amount of money in those days, especially for a man in his twenties. "I appreciate the offer," I said. "But, with the cancellation of this contract, my company is destitute. I'm not leaving a sinking ship. I'm going to stay with Dustbane."

"I knew you'd say that. But remember: this door is open. If you ever decide to work for somebody else, you come in that door because I want you." That was the last time I ever saw him. He canceled our contract because of a clash of personalities. He wouldn't be bulldozed by me and I wouldn't let him back away from his agreement.

At ten o'clock that morning I left Manville's office and went back to the furnished apartment where Stella and I were living. I told her glumly: "The contract is canceled and I don't know what to do." I lay down on the couch and, for the first time ever in a working day, fell asleep.

When I awoke at five I was a new man. There seemed no problems. I sent wires to all my key men and asked: "Do you want to come with me or stay with Manville?"

All the top men came. One top-notcher, L.A. Parker, was a young fellow I had picked up in a brush factory in Troy, New York. I wired him in Dallas, saying: "Meet me in Utica". I gave him just enough time and, when I arrived there he was on the platform waiting for me, having borrowed the train fare from a jobber. He stayed on with me as I built up a new Dustbane sales organization but became so outstanding that there was only one place left for him to go: into my job. Finally we met in Chicago and I said: "L.A. I'm going to fire you. You're too good; you really need my job. There's a wholesale grocer in Evansville who asked me to let him know if you ever left

Discovering Canada

me. Go to Evansville and join up with that grocer." I handed him a nice engraved gold watch, and said: "Let me know how you get along."

He joined that grocer and in two years owned the business. In ten years he was one of the richest men in Evansville, owning a wholesale grocery, a food brokerage, a bank, and a distillery. He used to beg me to come and visit him but I never went. Other men who knew him told me: "He takes this watch out and says that you made him what he is. He sings your praises."

By 1914 I had a salesforce of twenty and business was booming. We were grossing about $200,000, had eight people working in our factory in Ipswich, others in our Ottawa and Winnipeg factories.

Then came World War I, and the American government went to war with a vengeance, slapping embargoes on all "non-essential manufacturing". The government cut off our supply of tin (we sold Dustbane in cans for home use in cleaning carpets), then they cut off our supply of oil and we were virtually out of business.

Canada, however, applied no restrictions on oil or cans. I said to Green: "You go to Canada and look after the business there. I'll stay here and try to salvage the American operation."

Chapter 6

YEARS OF CONSOLIDATION
Playing straight pays best

It seems odd that Canada, which had been in the war two-and-a-half years longer than the United States would have fewer war restrictions. The reason, apparently, is that America was a principal supplier to the Allies long before she declared war and provided steel, copper, and cotton, as well as partly-finished and wholly-finished supplies. As a result, her industrial machine was already in top gear. Then, when Washington entered the war and needed to equip her own armies as well, she had to ration her resources so she could meet America's military and domestic needs as well as those of all her allies. Bernard Baruch headed up a War Industries Board which controlled exports and imports, railway traffic, shipping, materials, fuel, power, credit, construction. It was the efforts of this Board you ran afoul of.

I don't suppose you were the only one affected. Presumably by this time there were others in the sweeping compound business. Your success with Dustbane would surely have attracted competitors. Were the restrictions driving them to the wall too?

THERE'S ALWAYS COMPETITION. One firm in Chicago, one in New York were doing quite well making sweeping compounds and they were in the same predicament. Between us we had factories in Jersey City, Chicago, and Ipswich, and we all had our own offices; it seemed to me that we might all be able to survive if we cut our overheads by consolidating.

I'd had no dealings with Perolin Inc. of Chicago, but the New York firm was controlled by a fellow named Hahlo, whom I'd met occasionally. He was a very clever businessman, an ex-member of the New York Stock Exchange, a dyed-in-the-wool New Yorker. His way of doing business and mine couldn't have been further apart. Nevertheless I took the train to New York and walked in on him.

I asked him if his company could survive. He said he didn't know. I acknowledged that I was in the same boat. Then I suggested that we merge, bring in the Chicago company, slice overheads, and salvage what we could. He agreed immediately and we made a deal; he took preferred stock in the joint company and I took common. This meant I was taking almost all the risk; if I failed in my attempts to save these three companies and we were forced to liquidate he would have first call on the assets. But I was in no position to make a tougher deal because he had access to money; he could supply working capital and I couldn't.

We named our new enterprise the United States Sweeping Compound Company. I was president, he became secretary-treasurer. He was never active in the business; he'd show up at nine o'clock, stay five minutes at the office then walk out again, to spend all his time at the stock exchange until it closed at three.

While I struggled to preserve the consolidated company, Green worked in Canada. He did well and made good money, but things proved increasingly difficult in New York. I was drawing $5,000 a year — a salary level achieved by only two percent of the population in those days — and because of our lack of supplies I wasn't really able to earn it. One day I announced to Hahlo: "I'm going to Canada for the rest of the war. I'll take a year's leave of absence without salary. You try to hold out here until we get back in business." His eyes shone a little at that, and it was a glint not a tear that I saw there because he had always planned to beat me out of my equity. Of the three merged companies mine had been the most profitable and he was sure he could find a way to get possession of it. As he had the preferred shares, he figured the day would inevitably come when he could shake me loose from my common stock. That's the way those New Yorkers operate. I knew that.

Even so, I wanted to leave. I wanted to go some place where I could do business. Besides, my position was not as insecure as he thought because filed in the back of my mind was a little incident.

He had kept monkeying in the stock market even though, because of some earlier shenanigan, he'd been disbarred as a member and he always dealt through a bank in Jersey City. One day he invited me to lunch with a vice-president of that bank. When we arrived there the official was out so we waited in his office. Hahlo seemed very much at home there. He took a note from a drawer, made it out for some amount, turned it face down on the desk. When the vice-president arrived, he signed his name on the back of the note without even checking the amount. I wasn't going to forget that.

After my announcement to Hahlo I went home to the house we were renting in New Jersey and told Stella: "We're leaving for Canada on Friday." When she raised her eyebrows, I burst out: "Look. I have only three assets: my youth, my ability, and my health. I can't afford to squander any of them. Who knows how long this war will last? We're moving to Canada because I can *operate* there."

It was December. (Significant things in my life always seem to happen in December.) Stella packed the bags. We left all our furniture in the apartment and told the landlady that if she didn't hear from us soon she could sell it to pay the remaining rent. Neither of us suspected that Stella and I would never again live in a place with our own furniture.

On a cold merciless day we arrived in Ottawa with two hundred dollars — all the cash I could lay my hands on — and spent Christmas in an awful rooming house.

Stella, a dedicated Christian Scientist, had Christmas spirit but didn't say much about it because I had always been antagonistic about Christmas. The religious aspect meant nothing to me because my family had never been involved with churches. And I hated that business of giving presents. When I was little, every other kid had Christmas presents, but we were too poor so I might only get a ball of popcorn or an apple off the tree.

On this Christmas eve in two rented rooms — and holy smoke, it was cold! — adrift with two hundred dollars and no firm plans, I started thinking about how mean I had been and I went out and bought Stella a Christian Science bible. I also went to a butcher shop and bought a turkey. When Stella woke up next morning, prepared as usual to receive nothing, I gave her the bible! Coming from me, it could have been the universe. Every year after that I gave her something. Indeed I managed to find quite a lot of Christmas spirit in me.

With the festivities behind us, I had to plan a future. Green was obligated by our arrangement to let me into the eastern Canadian company, but he was doing so well I knew he didn't want me busting in. Nor did I want a showdown with him; I could bide my time for that. Stella and I took the remains of our two hundred dollars and headed to Winnipeg to try to buy the Western company back from Dunbar Hudson.

I knew Hudson liked me and that he was a tough businessman, but honest. We arrived in Winnipeg on the first of January, 1918, and Hudson and I celebrated the start of the year by making a very tough business deal.

I told him: "I'll pay you twice what you paid me for this company five years ago. I'll pay for it in eighteen months out of the profits that I make *in excess of* the profits you have been making so far."

"Fine," he said. "And if you fail to make *sufficient* extra profits I'll retain everything you do make." If I failed to make the last payment of even a nickel I would forfeit everything; he would keep the business plus all the money I had paid in installments.

Stella was as good a salesman as I was, so she and I both went out selling in an eighteen-month blitz to make all this money. We had one thing in our favor: there was virtually no income tax, so I could retain all the profits. And the deal wasn't quite as tough as it looked: simple manipulating could make the money available to pay Hudson. I could borrow it from the company, pay Hudson for his stock, then, as sole owner, declare a dividend to myself to repay the loan.

Stella came on the road with me and we drew only fifty dollars a week to pay expenses. For us both, it was quite a comedown. In the U.S. we were used to living in good hotels. Now we lived in rooming houses, and ate in cheap Chinese restaurants. Stella took it marvelously and backed me to the last ditch. She was the most unusual person, and knew exactly how to handle me. I was like a puppy dog in her hands.

I carried on the Western business for three years, happy as a clam because I had very limited responsibilities. My factory was an old shed with its roof caving in, and I had two men working there. I did all the selling, operated very economically, and was soon turning over all kinds of money.

But I still had a major business lesson to learn and Dunbar Hudson, watching over me in almost a fatherly way, was the man to teach it to me. One day he said: "You're a terrific business-getter. You can sell like nobody's business. But there's one thing that you overlook: a company can do all the business in the world, but it's still a failure if it fails to make a profit. In business the only measure of success is profit." From that time on I was profit-conscious because that was, indeed, the rule by which I would be judged a success or failure. My companies still work to a very careful profit margin. We will not cut prices and fall below that level. Nor will we let our prices slide up to create a much higher profit level.

With things rolling nicely, I went back to the States to salvage my American investment. After three-and-a-half years I turned up unannounced at Hahlo's office in Jersey City and said: "I want you to buy me out."

He laughed. "*Buy* you out! Why would I do that? You have no equity. My preferred stock is worth more than the company's assets. *Buy* you out? Fat chance!"

"I still want you to buy me out."

My confidence puzzled him. "You're wasting your breath."

"This company is insolvent," I said, "and I'm still its president. Unless you buy me out, I'm going to petition it into bankruptcy. And you can't stand the investigation of your affairs that would follow." I could still *see* that note on the bank vice-president's desk, and I still respected my gut-feeling that hanky-panky was going on. Perhaps I was skirting blackmail, but I only wanted my share of the money out of our business.

Hahlo didn't say anything for quite some time. Then he asked me if I would discuss it with his brother-in-law, a lawyer in New York City. I knew he was stalling, but I was happy to give him time to think through all the implications. I took the ferry, then strolled to the lawyer's office on Wall Street. After he and I chatted for a while, the phone rang. It was Hahlo. The conversation from our end: "Yes, I'm afraid he can. . . . Yes, he can. . . . He can do that too. . . ." He hung up, grinned at me, and said: "Go back and see him."

It was a nice day for ferry rides. Hahlo received me with open arms, and an open cheque book. I stated an equitable price (I never take advantage of a man I've got over a barrel), and he gave me everything I asked for. These sharp New York business men are very good at this sort of give-and-take. Even when you get the best of them they don't get mad at you. We parted the best of friends.

With that settled I went back to Winnipeg. My future would be in Canada. I became a British subject and ever since then I've considered myself completely a Canadian.

Green, who had built up a substantial business in Ottawa, was still a bachelor and now wealthy enough to lead the swinging life of a man about town, but it started to warp him. He spent half his time trying to stop three girl friends finding out about each other. It was none of my business except that I still owned a third of his company. One morning I received a telegram asking me to come to Ottawa.

When I arrived, Green looked terrible. He had lost his grip completely, was quite intoxicated, and the company was on the edge of bankruptcy. It was tragic. The man who had created the product, launched the company, helped me climb the business ladder, was now nothing but a liability. He pleaded: "Try to save the business."

I could have taken the company from him for nothing, but you don't kick a man when he's down. Instead I arranged to buy him out over a period. At the time I felt rather pleased with myself for "doing the decent thing". Years later, it paid unexpected rewards.

Now I owned both Canadian companies, but I still spent my time selling and traveling. President? Owner? Who cares about titles: the product had to be *sold*. I stayed on the road for twenty-seven years and loved it. Work has always been such pleasure to me that I hesitate to call it "work". I was so keen I alternated between Canada and the U.S. to bypass the public holidays. When it was a holiday in Canada, I sold in the States; on American holidays, I sold in Canada. Only Christmas and Good Friday stumped me.

Throughout those years, Stella stayed with me on the road. In Ottawa we lived right in the office. When we had to spend a month in a place, we'd take a furnished apartment. I wanted her with me for companionship, someone to talk to.

After some years I established my first branch operation; it was in Vancouver and employed three men. Its first year's financial statement proved this trio were stealing me blind. I couldn't catch the next train west to sort them out because my dear Stella was dying. A daring thought came to me. I went to find Green.

He was half-drunk in bed in the middle of the day. "G.W.," I said, "I want you to go out to Vancouver and get rid of those guys and take over."

A glint of hope flickered in his blurry eyes. "Do you think I can do it?"

"You can do anything that anybody else can do." He got up, straightened himself out in three or four days, and went to Vancouver. He threw out the local men, took over the business, and made a tremendous success of it for seven years. At fifty-six he married his twenty-year-old secretary and they had a son. When G.W. Green died, he was a respected citizen of Vancouver. A man who seemed to have shot his bolt, got out of bed and put in the seven best years of his life. All he needed was confidence. If I'd taken his equity for nothing he would not have trusted my judgement, not have gone to Vancouver. He'd have died a drunken bum, and I would have missed one of the greatest pleasures of my life.

Years of consolidation

Stella died in 1923. The following year I married Mildred, a company stenographer, and after that *she* traveled with me. With her, I could establish my office any place.

In 1929 I was visiting Green in Vancouver when I heard from Ottawa that a fire had gutted our factory. All the way back in the train I kicked and cursed myself for being under-insured. The building and contents were covered for their depreciated price, not their replacement value.

At the Bank of Toronto I had a $50,000 line of credit meant to be used strictly for current business. I'd always had an excellent relationship with the bank but now, for the first time, I put that in jeopardy by using my current credit to rebuild and re-equip my plant. Such a move is absolutely against bank policies because it ties up their money. They couldn't get their money out of me unless I sold my buildings and machinery. One day the bank summoned me to Toronto. They didn't *ask* me to come; they *told* me to.

John Lamb was vice-president of the bank (he became president in 1935), and he and his general manager and his supervisor of practices and some others were all waiting for me, and gave me hell for an hour. I didn't know if they were going to force me to sell or what they were going to do. Then they kept me there for a second hour and gave me advice. I listened. Carefully. I'm *always* prepared to listen to people who know what they're talking about. Then they said in effect: "Go on home, and don't do it again."

Instead of slinking out, I paused for a moment. "Mr. Lamb," I said, "I want to thank you. I've had two hours of time and advice from four of the top businessmen of Canada, all for free and all for my own good. This account can be nothing but a nuisance to the bank, yet you spent two hours trying to help me. I appreciate it."

"Do you mean that?" I nodded. "Nobody ever said that before," he noted.

From that time on my relations with the bank were always perfect. I worked hard to rebuild and then maintain their confidence. A good relationship with a bank is vital to a businessman.

The process of building up branches across Canada took a long time because I didn't want to bring in outside money. I used only my bank credit and never took more out of the company than I needed to exist. After G.W. Green straightened out my first branch in Vancouver, I used the profits on that to launch the next one. Outside money would have put me under an obligation to somebody and I didn't want to bother with anybody else. When I could have my own way entirely, I could move faster. And I wanted to keep moving.

Chapter 7

SPEAKING OF FAMILIES
The man's role: make money

You must have been a helluva husband! It seems you always put business first, family second. You're very independent, you hate both personal and business restrictions. Even in the last few years friends have called you "the only married bachelor" they know.

However you must be enthusiastic about marriage, because you married three times and you and your third wife are about to celebrate your fiftieth anniversary. During all those years you stayed on the road, you expected your wife to travel with you just so you'd have companionship. I can't imagine any woman enjoying a gypsy existence like that. Until you were past fifty you had no house you could call "home". I wonder whether, just as your messed-up childhood dehydrated Christmas for you, it also sucked any meaning out of the concept of "home".

EVERYONE NEEDS SOMEONE. No man is sufficient unto himself, and I've always felt the need of somebody, even though I'm not clear in my mind what that need is.

My first marriage was based on sympathy for Jenny who was having a very hard time, and she saw me as a solution to her problem. She was pretty, I was twenty. We were married at a minister's home one evening and I had to be at work at six the next morning to start the usual twelve-hour day.

Within a week I knew I'd made a mistake. She had no idea of housekeeping. When I came home the first night the beds weren't made and the dishes weren't washed. She'd read a book all day. On Sunday, my first day off after we were married, I cleaned the whole house. I thought she'd be ashamed to let me do it, but she thought it was great! She not only had a husband and security; she had somebody to do the housework. I had made a bad bargain.

My nine dollars for a seventy-two hour week couldn't support the three of us so I also tended furnaces before and after work. I got up at four o'clock, to look after the furnaces at five, and be on the job at six. After work I'd get the furnaces ready for the night then be home at nine o'clock. I was determined to make a success of the marriage and didn't complain. I set an example, hoping she'd get the idea. But she was quite happy to see me do the housework and never changed.

Over the years we drifted apart. There was never fighting between us. When I went on the road, however, naturally I took a look at a pretty waitress or a chambermaid. I was only twenty-six. I went on about my business until, on a boat trip from Saint John to Boston, I met Stella, who was separated from her husband. Although she was six years older than I was, we had a lot in common. Jenny and I were divorced and Stella and I were married in Kansas City by an old tobacco-chewing justice of the peace. We walked in, I gave him ten dollars, he mumbled a few words, and we walked out.

(Jenny and I had produced three daughters: Winifred, Madeleine, Gala. At fifteen Madeleine got married, and Winifred married young too. Gala came to me and attended Ottawa Ladies College, then went on to McGill University. Jenny divorced three husbands. In later years she lived in Florida and we became friends and used to visit back and forth. She has spent Thanksgiving and Christmas at our house.)

Stella and I were always very close. She was an outstanding person, everybody liked her and was charmed by her. She never said a mean word about anyone. When she died I thought for a while life wasn't worth continuing until I realized she wouldn't have wanted me just to shrivel up and wither away.

Mildred and I have had fifty good years together. She is like Stella in many ways: she too believes that if you can't say something kind about a person it's best to stay silent. We have two daughters, June and Marilyn.

Was I involved with my children? Not by modern standards. Money and security are the most important things a man contributes to a marriage. I was deeply concerned that my children should be able to stand on their own feet financially; I also wanted to give them the foundation that would let them fend for themselves. I was no doting father; no "companion" to them. On the other hand, I never fought with them, I never punished a child, and I talked to them a lot.

My policy was to reason. Children should have convictions of their own and not do things just because adults want them to. I never accepted the idea that children have to respect their elders. We "elders" have made such a mess of things that we're not entitled to respect. Today's young people, providing they put intelligence to work, have the opportunity to do a better job.

I'm a great admirer of success: I like to see people make something of themselves. I've had great pleasure in watching the progress of Gala who became president of Dustbane; of June who has a doctorate in psychology; and of Marilyn who has a master's degree in social work.

I don't believe young people should automatically get married. Marriage is no journey into inevitable bliss. It's a contract between two people who offer each other companionship, family, sympathy and understanding when they need it. It's a contract with obligations on both sides. People should study this before they get married.

Many women think that marriage ties down a man and that's all there is to it. Before marriage they put on a show for him, but then they stop. They should keep that show running, keep on fooling the man. I *want* to be fooled if it gives me pleasure and happiness. I want to be wooed as long as I live. A man is not naturally monogamous so it's a woman's responsibility to keep him hypnotized. If she fails to do so he faces a terrific temptation.

A husband's job is to look after the important things, to supply the necessities, make a success of his life, look after and educate the children. Marriages should have a written agreement outlining these responsibilities so that both parties understand what they have to do.

From the time I was a boy I believed that women are equal to men in every respect. All my working life I've placed women in responsible positions. I trained a woman to take over my job as president of the United Sweeping Compound Company of America. My daughter took over my job as president of Dustbane Enterprises. I believe in sharing all the work. When Stella worked alongside me I cooked and washed dishes and swept just as much as she did.

I'm sure it was *interesting* for my wives to travel! We'd live in Winnipeg for three months, Vancouver for three months, then Montreal, Toronto. It wasn't difficult to find a furnished apartment and set up housekeeping for a month or two. In Ottawa we took over the elaborate office Green had built and fixed it up as a bedroom and a kitchenette.

66 *Speaking of families*

I admit I don't have much of a home instinct. I can set up any place. And I can walk out of any place and forget it. When we went to Winnipeg, we left our home in Hoboken, New Jersey, and never saw the furniture again. I couldn't have cared less.

Even after I built up a sales organization, I always trained the salesmen in the field. Mildred keeps suitcases packed for me in case I suddenly decide to go somewhere. She has a case of warm clothes in case I go north to fish; a case of cool clothes in case I go to Florida.

In 1930, when Green died in Vancouver, I asked Roy Wellwood, a fine man working for me, to go out there and take over. He fell in love with Vancouver and after about eighteen months I asked him if he wanted to stay there. He said he'd like to but would have to dispose of his house in Ottawa. I told Mildred: "I have to take over this house of Wellwood's. I guess we'd better move in." That was the first home we ever had. I was fifty.

In the 1950s, Mildred decided she'd like a new home. I gave her a budget of $30,000 to buy a lot and design and build a house, and not tell me or ask me anything about it. I heard somewhere that she had started building so one day I drove over to the lot to peek. The house was coming along nicely but there was something peculiar about the garage doors. When I asked the builder about them, he said, "They're all your wife can afford. She won't go a penny over budget!"

I told him to do the job properly: another hundred dollars wouldn't put me in the poorhouse. When we moved in the garage doors worked fine.

But let me tell you more about my company . . . . .

In the 1920s we started to diversify. Then, as now, a businessman wanting to survive needed to anticipate change and adapt to it. Although Dustbane was grossing $150,000 a year and was very profitable, it was vulnerable. Change could make it obsolete. When we started selling sweeping compound there were only wooden floors, but now other types had come in, and Dustbane didn't work well on some of them. Its chemicals dissolved the binder in linoleum and the manufacturers included a warning with every roll: "Sweeping compounds not to be used on this surface." As linoleum became increasingly popular Dustbane might be in trouble. I decided to diversify into waxes and other cleaning substances. We were pioneers in that field too.

There were very few special sanitation products; no liquid soap, not even toilet paper. To produce soaps and waxes we had to teach ourselves how to make them. Even though I'm so hopeless with my hands, I'm pretty good with

Speaking of families 67

my head so I decided I'd be the one to learn and went to see a commercial chemist in Montreal. I shouted at him, because he was deaf: "I want you to teach me how to make soaps and waxes, but I don't want a general course in chemistry. I only want to know what I *have to* know." After he got the idea it appealed to him immensely and I started to spend every spare minute in his lab, with the two of us shouting back and forth. Within two or three months I knew enough about soaps to start manufacturing.

When I returned to Ottawa, I spoke to young Johnnie McCauley who was working in my factory. He had very little education — he could hardly read or write — but I taught him everything I had learned about making soaps and cleaners and then he took it from there. He became our "wax man" and always kept thoroughly up-to-date on the business. He remains one of the best soap production people in the world.

Most companies in soap and wax sell to housewives, but the industrial market has always appealed more to me. Consumer soap companies *can* be huge and profitable. Procter and Gamble sells hundreds of millions of dollars' worth of soaps and detergents every year. Colgate-Palmolive did $1,309,000,000 worth of business in 1971. In 1972 Lever Brothers sold more than a million cases of just one product, Sunlight liquid detergent, to consumers in Canada alone. But I *never* wanted to get into consumer marketing. It demands a lot of advertising, and a way of talking to customers that never appealed to me very much. Consumer soap marketing is aimed at women, not men, and the feminine market is altogether different. Without wanting to be murdered by the women of this world, I must say that logic doesn't seem to have a great deal to do with what they decide to buy. Companies such as S.C. Johnson spend about four million dollars a year on advertising in Canada. Lever Brothers spends about five million. And almost all that soap and detergent advertising is an attempt to pull the wool over people's eyes, to make them believe in magic products that can take the work out of cleaning. I don't believe in magic.

At Dustbane it's different. We sell our products to *men*. We can go out and *demonstrate* the qualities of our products. The industrial market is big enough to satisfy *my* ambitions. G.H. Wood Company is our biggest competitor in Canada and it's strictly an industrial marketer too, and there are a lot of smaller ones; nevertheless the companies we own or control have about sixty percent of the market.

In the 1920s the only wax known was paste wax in a mineral solvent. A little later emulsified water waxes appeared. I always made a point of keeping up with developments because I didn't want anything to get established without us being on the bandwagon; so I immediately made a deal to import emulsified water wax from a company in New York. That company eventually sold out to Franklin Research of Philadelphia and we got along well with the Franklin people and brought in their emulsified wax by the carload. Finally, however, the volume got so big that we decided to manufacture it ourselves in Canada.

It wasn't hard by that stage to get a satisfactory formula from a commercial chemist, but Franklin Research had looked after Dustbane for all those years and somehow it didn't seem right to cut them off, as I obviously could because we had the entire Canadian market tied up. I went to Philadelphia and said: "We've decided to manufacture wax ourselves. And even though I don't have to, I'm going to pay you a royalty of five cents a gallon for the way you've served me all these years."

That was the most surprising thing they'd ever heard of. (It sounds pretty surprising to me too in 1973!) They talked amongst themselves for a while then said: "Instead of offering to pay us five cents a gallon for nothing, how would you like to pay us fifteen cents a gallon for *something*? We're old-timers in this business and have a lot of know-how. We can provide you with technical services that will easily save you thirty cents a gallon."

We made a deal. That was thirty-six years ago and the deal is still standing. After Franklin Research was sold to Purex Corporation of Los Angeles, the world's largest manufacturer of detergents and waxes, we continued the relationship. We still pay Purex for technical services, and that lets us import or produce anything they perfect down there. We don't have to gamble in putting something new on the Canadian market until they have tried it out first. And that relationship all traces back to the feeling on my part thirty-six years ago that it would be unfair to cut Franklin off in Canada.

We went into the early years of the Depression grossing about $225,000 a year from the sale of sweeping compounds, waxes, and detergents. Through the Depression we showed no increase nor decrease; nor did we show a loss. Although we cut wages by ten percent, I was determined to get through without laying off one man and almost succeeded. In 1933 to avoid showing a loss, I laid off one man out of our fifty or sixty. He was George Armstrong, last-hired-first-fired. In 1936 when things got better again, Armstrong returned to us, became a traffic manager, then purchasing agent, and today still works half-days for Dustbane.

In the mid-thirties I saw a magazine advertisement for an electric floor polisher. I'd never heard of such a thing before; people polished floors with a weight on a handle. Vacuum cleaners had come into existence but their arrival hadn't bothered me because they were made for carpets and we sold only to big commercial buildings, none of which had carpets. A floor polisher, however, gave more cause for alarm. To protect Dustbane's long-term interests, I decided to learn more about this interesting device.

The best of such machines was the Finnell, so I wrote to the company and Mr. Finnell himself came up from Hannibal, Missouri. He was a tall man, dressed in black and wearing an odd sort of hat. He looked and talked more like a Methodist minister than a businessman. He was a fine man. We made a deal and maintained a relationship until he died in 1960. At first we imported his machines; later we arranged for him to manufacture them for us in Canada. We became the first to put electric polishers onto the market in Canada and sold hundreds, and then thousands, for industrial use.

Finnell was something of a genius but a dreamer, and eventually he lost control of his business. Before that happened, however, I saw the handwriting on the wall and decided I'd better manufacture independently. To set up machinery and equipment and dies for that was a huge step for a man who had originally started manufacturing with a whisky barrel and an electric motor! Today we're the largest manufacturer of industrial floor polishers in Canada and we make commercial vacuum cleaners as well. The Finnell company and its brand have disappeared, and there's a moral there: a businessman has to be careful to keep control of his company; and he always has to anticipate and prepare for change. No matter how big a company is, it can disappear as the dinosaur did if it does not adapt. I am determined that Dustbane will never disappear.

There certainly seemed no likelihood of us disappearing as we ended the 1930s: our gross had passed the million-dollar mark, and we'd never had an unprofitable year.

With Mildred,
his daughters Marilyn Wilson
and June Pimm,
son-in-law Gordon Pimm

With daughter Madeleine
and her son Jack

With his wife Mildred, his daughter June, her escort, Ed Fay

Chapter 8

POLITICAL CAREER

He was a cat among pigeons

Ottawa brought you success and happiness. You liked the place the moment you saw it; you had a home there for the first time; and it was there that you really prospered. By 1940 you were the sole owner of a business grossing $1,500,000 a year.

In those days the city had about 155,000 people and ran on a budget of about six million dollars. Unlike many world capitals, it was — and still is — self-governing, run by twenty-two aldermen and a four-man Board of Control.

You were living there when the federal government started its big building program in the second half of the 1930s; and in 1937 when the government brought in Jacques Greber, the French town planner, to begin the studies that led to the development of Confederation Square in the center of town. This was the time when the government put up the Justice building on Wellington Street; a postal terminal by Union Station; the Central Post Office; Supreme Court Building; Bank of Canada; National Research Council Laboratories; and in 1938 they razed the old post office to make room for the National War Memorial.

With all this planning and construction going on, and with the complex relationship that must exist between the city government and the federal government, it must have been very tempting for an aggressive and opinionated man such as you to get into politics.

POLITICS WAS TEMPTING. There was a lot to hold me back, however. I'm a capitalist, right? Well, the capitalist class has always been very selfish in taking things out of a community and not being willing to give much back. At the Rotary Club and the Laurentian and the Rideau I associated with my fellow capitalists, and the way they all talked about politics was very disturbing. They'd declare very confidently that all politicians were "dirty"; they'd pronounce, as if it were somehow virtuous, that you'd never catch *them* running for office.

Their attitude disturbed me. After all, a community is just like a business; it has to be *managed*. Ottawa couldn't have good schools and sidewalks and paved streets without somebody at the top paying attention. And who could be better at that than a businessman?

So I felt uncomfortable as my friends and associates kept declaring how they would have nothing to do with "dirty politics"! At the same time they all felt free to criticize the way the city was run, and to moan about high taxes and waste, implying that they personally *could* do a much better job, except of course they wouldn't soil their hands. I too could see that many things were done in an unbusinesslike way, and that there was waste; and I complained about it too, until one day it struck me that I should put up or shut up; be helpful or be silent.

I had one friend in local politics: Finley McRae. He had married a wealthy girl, so had no great working responsibilities, and no real outlet for his abilities so he ran for Board of Control.

Up to that time, I had never cast a vote in a civic election; I'd not been interested enough. On the day McRae ran, it seemed that the least I could do for my friend was to vote for him, but I couldn't find the right polling place. Twice I went to the wrong place. Quite fed up, I asked myself: "Why bother? Who needs the aggravation! One vote can't matter, and he'll never know." But my conscience nagged me. I went again to look for the polling place and this time found it. That night on the radio news I heard the results. The election was a tie! If I hadn't voted, McRae would have lost (as indeed he did lose on the recount).

Several times McRae told me that politics was interesting, and that I too should run for office, but I paid no attention. Then one Friday night in 1938, just after I arrived home from an eight-day hunting trip, I had a call from McRae who said in a brisk no-nonsense way: "Go to the firehall and take out your nomination papers."

"What on earth for?"

"Because you're going to run for alderman in Capital Ward."

"Capital Ward? Where's that?" I didn't know one ward from another! He carried on without waiting: "Bring along two citizens who are taxpayers in good standing to sign your papers and you're on your way."

I laughed at him: but the next morning I found myself thinking it over and I phoned my lawyer. "Come on down to the firehall. I'm going to take out my nomination papers." I still hadn't admitted to myself that I would run, but at least I'd have the papers.

Across the street from me lived Nelson Ogilvy, the City Clerk, and at six that evening he called me. "Are you serious?" he asked.

"Well, I took out my papers this afternoon."

"Then you have to 'qualify'. You have to come down here now and take an oath that you're fitted for public office. And if you're *not* down here before eight o'clock, your name won't be on the ballot." He spoke as if it were all a great joke; he couldn't *imagine* me running for office. Nevertheless I *went* down that night, *proved* that I owned property, *showed* my citizenship papers. I was running!

It was only then that I found out who I was running against: E.A. Band and Harold C. Marshall, in my opinion the only two good aldermen on city council. H.C. Marshall, in particular, a grocery broker and a substantial citizen, was the council's outstanding man.

Next day at lunch at the club everyone kidded me. I would take a terrible beating, they said; and I agreed. Even Harold Marshall was friendly and sympathized with me. Everyone knew I had no chance.

The election was only a week away. I couldn't stand the thought of making speeches and public appearances and was prepared to try only one campaign idea. In those days, long before ballpoint pens, everyone needed a good supply of blotting paper, so I printed thousands of high-quality blotters carrying my picture and name and just one line: "A change would do no harm". I sent Dustbane people to the schools to give all the kids a blotter as they left. It wasn't exactly sophisticated, yet those kids were so tickled that they went home and hounded their parents. A friend told me later: "My son came home with your blotter and harped and harped until I went to the polls to vote for you."

On election day I sent Dustbane people to the polling places as scrutineers, and for the second time I voted in a civic election. Thus I knew I had one vote: my own. After the polls closed the first call I received was from our scrutineer at the place where I'd voted. He read out the results very slowly: "Band 92.... Marshall 104...." Then he stopped. I thought: "That's funny. Where's that vote I cast for myself?" Then he added: "... Pickering 147." It was unbelievable. Capital Ward gave Band 2,760 votes, Marshall 1,933 votes, and Pickering 2,615! Top two won.

I was elected on the strength of those blotters. How else? Nobody knew me. I'd never been in public affairs. That was my first indication of the idiocy of the election system. In later years I was to receive many others. Harold Marshall was so upset I don't think he ever went to the Laurentian Club again.

So now, rather unexpectedly, I was an alderman and I figured my chance had come to do some useful work for Ottawa. I imagined I'd have no trouble getting my ideas through Council because everything I wanted to do was constructive. That's when I learned my first political lesson. Most aldermen didn't want anybody to do anything. They didn't want some newcomer praised for his achievements; that just meant extra competition in the next election. They saw a threat in any upstart like me getting ahead. The curse of the political system is this obstruction from "little" people of little ability and vast jealousy.

My first frustration came over a matter of water. Ottawa supplied filtered water to various nearby municipalities and to the Federal government which paid 16.5 cents a thousand gallons. I asked the waterworks commissioner what it cost to filter the water. He didn't know!

I couldn't believe it. They were selling a product yet didn't know its cost! "That," I suggested to him, "is a damned funny way to do business." I ordered him to find out what it cost. That's when Council learned that filtering cost 20.5 cents a thousand! We were selling our product at a loss. At the next meeting I moved that we notify the federal government that, in future, we'd bill them for filtered water at cost. It seemed surely a logical and non-controversial idea, yet it ran me head-on into debate with the mayor.

Mayor Stanley Lewis was a very popular fellow and I always liked him, but his policy was to avoid mistakes by avoiding action. That approach, of course, fitted nicely in Ottawa, a city of civil servants who, in those days at least, were cautious people interested in progress and terrified to raise taxes. We all loved Lewis, but his approach worried me: I thought he might wreck

Political career

the city by avoiding progressive businesslike policies. Lewis, for his part, must have instinctively felt that, as the first big businessman to enter Ottawa politics, I challenged the civil service mentality, and thus challenged him. When I presented my motion about the water, he ruled it out of order. I was flabbergasted.

I couldn't accept his decision. I rushed to *The Ottawa Citizen* and told its publisher that I wanted to buy a full-page advertisement to put the facts before the people of Ottawa. "Hold on, hold on," he said. "We're delighted to sell advertising space, but there's a different way to go about this." He took me through to the editorial department and we discussed the situation with some writers, then they sent their auditors to city hall to check the figures I was using. Two days later they phoned to say: "You're right about the water; and we're going to give it full editorial coverage. Which won't cost you a cent." At the next meeting of council my motion went through without opposition.

I should have learned a lesson from that, and cultivated friends on the newspapers which have a terrific influence in Ottawa affairs. Lewis understood that very well; he visited the newspaper offices almost every day.

I had bad luck with one newspaper. Somebody phoned and woke me one night to say there was a dead cat on his street and that I should send a truck to pick it up. That seemed to me a damned silly way to waste taxpayers' money. I told him to pick it up himself and sling it in his garbage. Years later I learned that my caller that night was the editor of the *Journal*. From then on, the *Journal* was always tough on me.

After my first term as alderman, I ran again and was elected with 2,372 votes to Band's 2,562. All told, I ran twice for alderman, twice for controller, and twice for mayor and I hated every single campaign. To get elected you have to kowtow to people, to humble yourself before them as if to ask favors. Thus the very process of democracy undermines the honesty you want in your politicians. No one ever tried to get me as a politician to do anything unethical or dishonest; yet I had to be a hypocrite at election time by fawning over people.

I was always defeated in the working men's districts. On election days my opponents put people on street corners to tell people not to vote for me because I had too much money. My ability had nothing to do with how these people voted; it was more a matter of whether they liked the way I combed my hair. If I wanted to get elected, I had to go down there and buy beer and put on parties. Every politician had his henchmen, who'd make a few dollars by organizing house meetings with sandwiches and beer for fifty or seventy-five people. All that counted was the beer I bought and the hands I shook. I had to make those people in Lower Town think that I had no aim in life except to see that they got everything they wanted. Promise them everything, give them nothing, seemed to be the political rule.

After a few such campaigns I was starting to agree with my fellow-capitalists who said politics is "dirty". Not dirty really, but decidedly grubby. To stay in office, men have to practice things that are distasteful to them. But it is only in that sense that politics is "grubby". There was no graft in Ottawa.

After my second election, I had many more turn-ins with Stanley Lewis because I was moving up in the hierarchy now. I was ambitious and wanted to get things done and, in my impatience, I sometimes tried to push people out of my way. Impatience led me into many mistakes. Lewis, who was elected continuously for eight years, was never so impatient that he made mistakes. My biggest mistake was trying to push Lewis out of my way. If I had been more patient, I would have accomplished my objectives better. When I was elected to Board of Control I headed the poll. Then I was re-elected. So then I decided to get some real action for me and for Ottawa and I ran against Lewis for mayor.

Big mistake. I was put in my place. Even my own friends turned against me. "Why do you want to put him out of office?" they asked. "He's a nice guy; he doesn't make waves; he keeps the taxes down."

I made a public proposition. "Let's divide the office of mayor in two," I said. "Let's have a business mayor and a social mayor. Lewis can be the social mayor and lay cornerstones and meet visiting dignitaries and get all the glory. I'll be the business mayor and run the city on a businesslike basis." I didn't want to be called "Your Worship" and all that stuff. No one believed that I meant it, but I did.

In defeat, I managed to make the whole city mad at me. I was bewildered; I'd worked so hard and it seemed so unfair. My resentment got the upper hand on me. Whereas it's customary for the defeated candidate to make some gracious speech over the radio, I lost my head. I blurted out: "The people of Ottawa don't think they need me, and I don't think I need them. Goodbye."

Nobody likes a sorehead. It wasn't until years later, after I had done all sorts of voluntary unpaid community jobs that Ottawa forgave me that outburst.

I ran for mayor twice and Lewis defeated me both times. Then Charlotte Whitton ran against me for Board of Control. She is an outstanding woman, with tremendous ability, energy, and flair. I had always won a big vote from women but when Charlotte ran the women all ganged up to elect her. People are supposed to vote for four controllers but the women "plumped" for Charlotte Whitton; that is, they voted for only one person, so she swept in with twice the votes of any man in the field. If the women had voted for four candidates I'd have swept in too.

That defeat ended my political career except for one occurrence. Years later I ran for the Liberal federal nomination in Ottawa West. It was a joke. I knew I couldn't win because my opponent, George James McIlraith, was the leader of the local party. I ran because the party in that riding had slipped into a trough and nobody even bothered turning up for its conventions. When the newspapers heard I was running they ran headlines. They knew I'd be defeated and figured I'd probably get mad again and run as an independent.

That year the nominating convention was packed. Lester Pearson sat next to me at the head table and confided: "This is the best thing that's ever happened to Ottawa West. You've woken 'em up."

I did it out of deviltry and I had a lot of fun. In the election I voted for George McIlraith.

Chapter 9

DOING GOOD WORKS
Honorary chairman of everything

All that political hassling took place thirty years ago, but even then you were no spring chicken.

In 1941 you turned sixty. Your business was thriving; you'd been in and out of politics; the time had come, surely, for you to sit back and fish and travel and enjoy your money. But instead of quitting, you took on all sorts of unpaid community work.

Between 1940 and 1947 you served as chairman of the Ottawa War Salvage Committee; chairman of the Ottawa-Hull Citizens Rehabilitation Committee; member of the Local Employment Advisory Committee; first vice-president of the Eastern Ontario Flying School; president of the Ottawa Board of Trade; member of the executive of the Better Business Bureau; chairman of the board of arbitration that settled a dispute between the firefighters and the city; chairman of the Ottawa Committee for the National Clothing Collection for Overseas War Relief; president of the Laurentian Club; director of the Ottawa Football Club; Hydro Commissioner: chairman of the Welfare Fund Campaign for the Ottawa Community Chests; chairman of the Citizens' Housing Committee; chairman of the fund-raising campaign for the Canadian Council for Reconstruction; trustee of Ottawa Civic Hospital. That's quite a list.

Some businessmen take on these community jobs for the sake of their companies' public relations; others for altruism; some through guilt over their own wealth. Most, do it, I suppose, for a mixture of all these motives.

84   *Doing good works*

Your background, however, includes a couple of extra ingredients that may have influenced you. There was your determination from the start that you would "be someone"; that, unlike your father, you would not fritter away your time or talents. And there's another element. Perhaps because of your rough background, you have kept some sense of objectivity about business and businessmen, and you can admit to flaws in the way capitalism is practiced. I have a feeling that you took on all those voluntary jobs to hint to the world that you weren't exactly the same as so many of your fellow members of the businessmen's clubs.

I FELT A DEBT. I always had the feeling that I owed the city something because I'd grown rich in that community. I quit politics because I was discouraged by that process of having to beg people for their votes, but I didn't quit public life. In seven years I held nearly every office in the city of Ottawa, and from the beginning of the war I was head of Rehabilitation and also of a school for training pilots. I was keeping my business going too.

There's a saying: "When you want a job done, give it to a busy man". I've always liked getting things done, yet somehow I always seemed to have plenty of time. I never *felt* overworked. Even the local Chinese community and the Salvation Army asked me to be chairman of their fund-raising drives. I built a reputation for getting results, so they kept handing me these jobs. I kept accepting them until I was seventy-five and figured I could quit.

During the war the government asked people to do what they could to help various causes. One involved salvaging waste paper and tires and iron, and someone asked me to organize the collection in Ottawa. "Chairman of Salvage" they called me. I called on the school children. If they could talk their parents into electing an unknown to council, maybe they could achieve a more worthwhile goal. I organized a collecting competition between schools. The kids made little hand wagons for hauling the stuff to school, then we sent trucks to pick it up from there. Of course I had to make a few rousing speeches to help it all along. "Anyone who burns paper is committing an act of sabotage," I declared. "Loyal citizens, willing to support our fighting men, will see that paper is reconverted into salvage if they have to carry it to the salvage depots on their backs." The speeches or the kids or both or *something* made it all work. In four-and-a-half years in Ottawa, on bicycles and in hand carts, school children gathered 2,433,351 pounds of salvage. We even collected old bones which we sold for thirteen dollars a ton.

That success impressed a few people and when UNRA launched a drive for clothes for the destitute in liberated countries, I was again appointed chairman for Ottawa. And again I used school children as my chief collectors, and again I made some rah-rah speeches. "The people of Ottawa are parting with sentimental clothing," I declared. "It's clothing treasured by the women of families as tender reminders of departed ones, clothing that once belonged to grown children when they were babies, clothing that husbands once cherished in their lifetimes and which had been kept as mementos since their death. These donations are frequently new, have been daintily packed, and some still exude the perfume of trunks in which they have been delicately stored. The people of Ottawa are among the most humane and patriotic in the land, and nothing has brought this out more than the present clothing drive. . . ."

The Ottawa collection nearly topped the entire country. When the next clothing drive was launched, I was appointed *national* chairman. I organized the collection from coast to coast and that year, in pounds of clothing collected per head, Canada topped the world.

Next I became national chairman of the United Nations appeal for money to help children in wartorn countries. The organizing costs alone involved tens of thousands of dollars. I had to work with the best-known people in each province. Canada collected more cash per-capita than any other nation in the world except Denmark.

I was a member of the Regional Board of Unemployment Insurance. Anyone in a hassle with the government about unemployment could come before our review board which comprised a lawyer, a businessman, and a labor man. I was the businessman, but was frequently accused of being pro-labor.

Arbitration was compulsory in wage disputes during the war and the government appointed arbitrators with as much authority as a judge to handle some cases. The minister of labor asked me to be arbitrator in a dispute between the city and its firemen. We sat for five days, at the end of which it was quite obvious what was fair and equitable: as always in such disputes, it lay somewhere between what the firemen asked and what the city wanted to pay. In my "court" I could make my own rules so, after five days, I took the city lawyer and the firemen's lawyer into my office and said: "You've heard the evidence and you know what's right. I'm going to leave you together to come to an agreement. If you don't reach one, I'll make you." Within half an hour they were in agreement. A lot of labor disputes could be handled that way, simply by saying: "You guys do what's right, and do it voluntarily."

I was chosen to head the rehabilitation committee by General Burns, an outstanding man with a brilliant war record, who was serving as Assistant Deputy Minister of Veterans Affairs. (Ten years later, he became the first Chief of Staff of the United Nations Truce Supervision Organization in the Middle East.) He was a taciturn man. Once when a press photographer asked him to smile for the camera, he snorted: "I *am* smiling, damn it!" Burns approached me when the Department of Veterans' Affairs ran into difficult cases in its attempts to rehabilitate returned men. Some were suspicious of psychiatrists or social workers who tried to help them. They had a feeling that professionals of any sort were out to pull the wool over their eyes. When the Department couldn't get through to these paranoiacs, it decided to refer them to civilian committees. Burns asked me to be chairman for the Ottawa district. We all went through a four-day training session at the Seignory Club, then were turned loose to work it out.

I set up subcommittees of every church and ethnic group in the city — Catholics, Jews, Irish — people who might get close to these men. As difficult veterans appeared, the Department sent them and their case histories to me. I screened them all — two or three a day — then referred them to the appropriate subcommittee. Sometimes just our first conversation sorted things out.

Years after the war I was heading north on a fishing trip in a private plane when the pilot invited me forward. Over the roar of the engine, he told me: "It's thanks to you that I'm your pilot today." When I looked puzzled, he continued: "I was one of the veterans you talked to after the war. You advised me then to take a flying course, and here I am."

Through the rehabilitation work I got involved in an even more challenging assignment. There was a very serious housing shortage and many of the returning men were living under conditions that were unfair to any man who had risked his life for his country. In those days the Communists were trying every trick they knew to undermine our system of government and they had the bright idea of agitating among these veterans, to inflame their resentment against the government for failing to provide housing. One man they influenced was an excitable ex-pilot named Frank Hanratty. He persuaded homeless veterans to seize some barracks that were being converted to housing. Then they seized other public buildings and the idea spread through the country. Veterans seized a hotel in Vancouver; they just moved in and refused to budge.

General Burns said to me one day: "This situation is out of control. The Royal Canadian Mounted Police have clear proof that the Communists are deliberately fomenting this, but we can't get them out into the open. We have to maintain law and order, yet the city police can't do anything, because the public wouldn't stand for clobbering veterans. This has to be handled differently. We think they might trust a civilian committee." He asked me to head up such a committee with full authority to deal with the housing crisis.

I paused before answering. It was a very tricky challenge and a short cut to getting every group in town mad at me again. I asked General Burns if the mayor would appoint me with full authority to find, create, and allocate housing in the city. And that's what happened: my old friend and opponent Stan Lewis appointed me head of the Emergency Housing Committee.

Then I went to see the head of the RCMP. He showed me the confidential files so I knew whom I had to smoke out. I negotiated with government departments to convert empty barracks to emergency housing but, as fast as we did this, Hanratty's Veterans' Housing League moved in. His fast-hitting mobile forces seized housing at Kildare Barracks, HMCS Carleton, Porter's Island, Lansdowne Park.

In trying to outmaneuver Hanratty, I had to be very careful because he had the sympathy of the people. I appointed a committee representing all the organizations of Ottawa and asked him to serve on it. He agreed to, and also said he'd bring all future emergency cases the League knew about to the Committee. But he was a suspicious man and, at the very first meeting, he and I nearly came to blows. I could report making real inroads into the problem and promised the meeting that every emergency case would be housed by November 4th. Hanratty kept talking and interrupting and declaring that he had eight hundred needy people requiring homes and that our projects would never be ready on time.

When I called a public meeting in the Lord Elgin Hotel, Hanratty trooped in with about a hundred men and women, all claiming they were veterans who couldn't get houses. As I watched them all troop in, I made an instant decision. I ordered all the doors locked. Then I said: "I want the name and number and regiment of every man in this room. You won't get out until I have it. I also want a description of the conditions you're living in." That action changed them from a mob, with all the irresponsibility of being anonymous, into a group of named individuals. The meeting became very orderly. Afterwards I took the names to the Welfare Department and put its staff investigators to work. Two days later they brought me back information about the people on the list. Of the hundred protesters, only four or five were genuinely destitute or homeless. I then took the Welfare Department's information to the *Ottawa Journal* which published it on the front page. The demonstrators immediately lost the public's sympathy and I had won my battle. The Communists grew so exasperated that one party member gave an open interview to the *Journal* bragging about what they were still going to do. The *Journal* published that on its front page too and the whole thing fizzled out.

Later, Hanratty came to my office and admitted he'd made a fool of himself. No one would give him a job. When I hired him for Dustbane, that titillated the newspapers some more. He wanted to become a journalist and, after he'd worked for me for a while, *The Citizen* gave him a job. He did well after that. Every four or five years he calls me and reports his progress. The last I heard he was editing a newspaper in the Maritimes.

During the years that I handled those big community jobs I had a very up-and-down relationship with the press. I remember a turn-in with P.D. Ross, editor of the *Ottawa Journal*. He was chairman of the Hydro Commission and Frank Plant, one of the two other commissioners, was rather a pet of his. Plant was an ex-mayor of Ottawa and I never liked him, but P.D. Ross seemed to think he was the cat's whiskers.

When friends of mine in city council wanted to do something for me, to show their appreciation of my work for the city, they replaced Plant with me. I had no hand in their decision but I was willing to accept the appointment because I knew it would be an interesting job. The *Journal* came out with a biting editorial denouncing city council. Ross wrote that, as a result of my appointment, he had already sent in his resignation from the Commission. The implication was quite clear: I was some sort of animal he didn't want to associate with.

Now I was a prominent businessman with some standing in the community and this irritated me, especially as I had never met or seen P.D. Ross in my life. I marched into his office. "Mr. Ross," I said, "I'm upset about that editorial. Perhaps it has some substance to it, and I don't realize it. I came down here to let you straighten me out. If I am the kind of man you're hinting at, I want to change. Perhaps you can tell me how to be different."

He stared at me, then took his paper and re-read the editorial, then looked embarrassed. "Mr. Pickering," he said finally, "I don't know you. I have never met you. I have nothing against you." He was upset now, because he was an honest and decent man. He'd written that editorial without thinking through its implications. Then he said: "I don't want you to leave until I rectify this. I can't rectify the publicity, because once that gets away you never catch up with it. But I can withdraw my resignation." He phoned Toronto and did that while I was sitting there. Then he wrote another piece for the paper confessing that he had nothing against me and had no reason to resign as far as I was concerned, and that he would continue to serve.

After that the *Journal* was always scrupulously fair to me. When I was elected president of the Board of Trade, its editorial declared: "Mr. Pickering has the time and, fortunately for his community, the inclination and the ability for public service. He has worked for Ottawa ... with the wholehearted zeal and the keen intelligence which, applied to his private business, gave him the leisure he is using so splendidly for the public advantage. A community is rich in the possession of men like Mr. Pickering and the Board of Trade is to be congratulated on the election of a man with so much business experience, administrative competence, and public spirit."

Several years later, City Council replaced me as Hydro Commissioner, in a secret vote, just as they'd earlier replaced Plant. The *Journal* trumpeted: "Not a shadow of excuse exists why the City Council should oust as commissioner a citizen of the high character and fine public record in many respects of C.E. Pickering...The seventeen members of the City Council who voted at the recent secret meeting to oust Mr. Pickering from the Hydro Commission did a thing injurious to the public interest — for good public service deserves support from the rest of us — and discreditable to themselves, indeed, rather shameful."

Charlotte Whitton and I had some great turn-ins, after she beat me for Board of Control. Dr. Whitton has been famous in Ottawa for years and she deserves all her fame. What a woman! She grew up in a small town in the Ottawa Valley and was always highly competitive. As a kid she once worked night and day to win a newspaper subscription campaign that offered a piano as first prize, even though her family already had a piano. She won the contest alright and gave her prize to the local Legion. Later she won six scholarships to Queen's University and, when she graduated, was the most brilliant student of her time, tops in several sports, editor of the college paper. In Ottawa she served fourteen years as controller and alderman, then was mayor for six consecutive terms.

She was always a fighter and caused endless controversy in council with her outspokenness and enthusiasm. Ernie Jones, a longtime alderman and controller, was needling her about something one day when Charlotte pulled a pistol on him. It turned out to be only a water pistol but the story appeared in newspapers in half-a-dozen countries. She was about to be appointed ambassador to Ireland but that controversy killed the appointment. She was clever and likeable but she fought hard. As mayor, she was a member *ex officio* of the Civic Hospital Board when I was chairman and she opposed everything I wanted to do.

They were exciting, productive days and I reveled in the atmosphere of working and achieving worthwhile things, of being where the action is. Then on Dominion Day, 1946, I was resting over the long weekend at our country place when my daughter Gala telephoned from Ottawa. "Congratulations," she said, "on your honor."

"What honor?"

"Didn't you know? It's in this morning's paper. You've been awarded the Order of the British Empire!" I'd never expected anything like that.

Queen Mary, head of the Order, signed her name to the proclamation, and the Governor-General, Viscount Alexander of Tunis, made the presentation at Government House. I was very proud, very aware of my background as a country boy who had once been an outsider in this country. I still have the ribbon and medal but I never wear it.

With Princess Alice

Captain Hyman, C.E. Pickering, Field Marshall The Viscount Alexander of Tunis, Redverse Pratt, Colonel Cavey

Chapter 10

CONTRACT CLEANING

New field, new worries, new hopes

You couldn't stay out of the thick of things, could you! When you were sixty-eight you ran in yet another election and put in two more years as a controller; and all this time you were still running your business. I can't understand how you found the time, let alone the energy at sixty-eight, to do all these things. You must have been on the run sixteen hours a day. Didn't you ever take time off for fun? What's the use of being successful and prosperous if all you do is work?

WHY CALL IT WORK? Sometimes I think I haven't done a day's work in my life: how *can* it be "work" when I enjoy it so much! And of course, I had fun. Lots of it. Wait 'til I tell you about some of the parties we had and the trouble we got into. I've always been a horse enthusiast and took every chance I could to go to the racetrack. I timed most of my business visits to Toronto to coincide with the race season; I got up early every morning to finish my work, then slipped out to Woodbine in the afternoon. Horses have been my great love ever since those days in Worcester when I wanted to drive the "smartest team with the shiniest harness". Even today I spend about two hundred afternoons a year at the track.

Back there twenty and thirty years ago I always found time for horses and politics *and* work. Part of the secret is that I know how to delegate. The way to keep your time and mind free and to keep things going, to accomplish a lot and still have a chance to stay creative, is to delegate, to get other people to carry out your plans after you've thought of them. I don't *waste* time, but I'm never short of it.

By the time I was seventy I had a good team of managers at Dustbane. Best of them was my daughter, Gala. She was always a brilliant girl and graduated in arts from McGill University in Montreal. A B.A., however, doesn't qualify a girl for anything much except being "a lady" and Gala couldn't see herself playing ladies all her life. She told me in the 1930s that she wanted to work for me.

"How can you do that?" I asked. "You have no qualifications." Then I added: "But if you'll go to business college now, I'll give you a job in my branch in Montreal. (I don't want you around here upsetting the head office organization because you're my daughter.)" So in 1936 she joined Dustbane as a junior clerk in Montreal at thirty-five dollars a month and quickly became the best clerk we had there. Earning her way every step, she moved from junior clerk in Montreal, back to head office, then along the line to more and more important positions. Within ten years she was head of the accounting department, and eventually she became president.

Meantime the business grew steadily but not spectacularly and reached about four million dollars a year. It was healthy, steady, profitable, almost entirely owned by me, and making $300,000 or $400,000 a year which I ploughed back in. Just what it was worth as an asset is hard to say. Today you generally multiply earning power by about fifteen to arrive at an asset value, so, on that basis, Dustbane was then worth about five million dollars. However, those days of quiet, unspectacular growth were about to scatter behind us like thistledown. I was going to start a new business.

The way I got into contract cleaning shows again how important luck can be. In 1954, at the age of seventy-three, I spent the winter in Los Angeles, watching the horses, having a drink, taking life easy. One day I decided to visit Knotts' Berry Farm, a well-known tourist attraction and on the way there by taxi I passed a building with a big sign showing a janitor with a pail and a mop. "I should visit that place," I thought. "Maybe I can pick up some ideas." At the time I couldn't be bothered, but the memory of the place kept niggling at me until finally, almost against my will, I took a taxi out there.

I asked for the manager and introduced myself. "I'm Pickering from Canada," I said. "I'm the head of a company called Dustbane Products." He knew all about me and Dustbane! He said he'd been thinking of getting in touch with me! Then he told me about his business which turned out to be quite foreign to anything I knew. He called it: "contract cleaning". When he showed me lists of his cleaning accounts, including three in Vancouver, I paid very close attention. He said he was thinking of using Dustbane as a supplier for a new coast-to-coast cleaning company he planned to build in Canada.

On the surface his proposal looked quite good — we could sell a lot of products to and through him — but alarm bells were chiming in my head. His mistake as a businessman was that he talked too much: indeed he *kept* talking until I finally awoke to the danger I was in. If I let him build this coast-to-coast business and he controlled the contracts, then he could replace me with any other supplier any time he liked, and at that stage Dustbane would be almost instantly out of action. There'd always be plenty of companies around prepared to underbid Dustbane to get such a large piece of business. I realized now that I didn't want this man to get established in Canada at all! I had to take quick action.

I told him I wanted to bring more of my people in to discuss it, then high-tailed back to my hotel. There I phoned Dave Hyman, my right-hand-man in Ottawa. "Grab a plane immediately. I want you here tomorrow," I said. I didn't even tell him why. Next day, we went out to the plant together. "I've brought my general manager down from Canada," I explained. "I'd like you to tell him your story too." He was delighted to do so and went into it now in even more detail because he was convinced he was on his way to a deal. Then Dave and I returned to the hotel. "I want you to get back on a plane now," I said, "and go to Winnipeg. And immediately start a contract cleaning business there." Within a week Dave was in business. Within three weeks I was back in Canada and had formed a totally new division: Modern Building Cleaning Services. Today that division accounts for two-thirds of Dustbane's total volume and three-quarters of its profits.

I moved into that new operating area because I could see that, as contract cleaning spread, the existing market for my products would partly disappear. I was right in that. Today a large percentage of Dustbane products — millions of dollars worth — are sold to and through Modern. If I had fallen into that Californian's perfectly honest and legitimate trap, he, not I, would today dominate cleaning in Canada.

The relationship between contract cleaning and the supplies and equipment business is an interesting one. If people who own buildings invested enough money to buy Dustbane's very best equipment and supplies, they might maintain their premises for less money than it costs to hire Modern to do it. But most owners won't invest the $5,000 or so it costs for the right machinery.

The first thing *we* do when offered a cleaning contract is survey the building then put in the very best equipment to do the job. We don't cut a single corner because the more good equipment we use the lower our labor costs will be. We are prepared to *invest,* so we can do the job better and therefore we get and keep the contracts. Modern buys nothing but the best, and it buys it all from Dustbane.

I never saw that Californian again. He later tried to expand in Canada but couldn't against us because we were already established too strongly. Outside of Vancouver, we've fenced him off.

Modern's first two years were difficult. I couldn't have Hyman run the new company because he was tied up with Dustbane. At first I brought in an experienced fellow from New York and gave him a very liberal contract. If he'd had the sense to do the job he was capable of, while also following the principles of business that I laid down, he'd have been a rich man today. Instead he got impatient. He thought he could elbow me out, then start his own company built on my contracts. Again I was saved by luck.

E.S. Sherwood, a big real estate owner with whom we did business, was quite a good friend of mine. One day my manager from New York went to him and suggested they use all the cleaning contracts Sherwood had placed with Modern to form the base of a new company. That New Yorker took for granted that Sherwood would happily sell me down the river in order to save a few dollars because that's the way they do business in New York. Instead my friend stalled him, then later called me over. "Do you know what's going on?" he asked. "This fellow plans to organize a new cleaning company. He wants me to go in with him."

"Did you turn him down?"

"Not yet. I thought I might be handy to you."

"You will be. Why don't you phone him now and let me listen in on the extension."

That's what he did. My man, now convinced he had a deal going, spelled out the whole plan while I listened in. Later I called him in to my office and said: "You walked into a trap." I fired him of course, but there was no real rancor between us. He went back to New York, joined a large contract cleaning firm there, and made good. I see him in New York sometimes and we've even been fishing together.

I went back to New York and hired another man trained in contract cleaning but he, too, had that unscrupulous way of doing business. It seemed quite

Contract cleaning 97

proper to him to get a contract on a cut price, then later trim services to try to wring a profit out of it. The first big important contract he won for us in this way was for Malton Airport in Toronto.

One day, flying back to Ottawa from New York, I changed planes in Toronto. Naturally I inspected the airport, expecting it to be up to our standards of maintenance. It was filthy! I went promptly to the superintendent and told him he had the dirtiest airport in North America. "And what damn business is that of yours?" he asked. I told him. Then I asked him to show me the cleaning contract and I could see immediately that we couldn't do a proper job at that price and still make a profit. I canceled the contract. Before we withdrew, however, we made that building immaculate.

Between them, those New Yorkers gave me all kinds of trouble and Modern got deeper and deeper into a mess. It lost $60,000 or $70,000 during that time. However a new bright star was about to show on my horizon, and it would light my way to a much happier future.

Chapter 11

INTRODUCING LAFORTUNE
How to pick a president

At the time you were having all this trouble launching Modern Cleaning Services, Gala was president of Dustbane and you were chairman and chief executive, right? You were still whooshing through life like a shot from a fieldgun. Although you told us that you believe totally in delegation so that you can stay free and creative and alert to opportunities and dangers; yet you hadn't really laid down the reins. Was it proving hard to step aside? As an entrepreneur who had built his own company from scratch, did you resent the idea of handing it over to younger "professional managers"?

It was at around this period of Dustbane's growth that Gerry LaFortune, who would eventually become president and chief executive, started to move up in the ranks. Looking at the situation from the outside, it's hard to see anything in LaFortune's background that would let you pick him as a likely winner. He was a young bookkeeper who had been studying to enter the priesthood, and a great tennis-player, and that's about all that was known about him. What was it that you spotted in him?

THE TALENTS OF LAFORTUNE: I don't know how I was lucky enough or smart enough to spot them. He joined Dustbane in 1947 when he was twenty-one and worked with Phillip Tetu, our secretary-treasurer. Mr. Tetu had been with us a long time, starting in 1920 as office manager and for years he was my mainstay. In some ways he was more responsible for my success than any other individual. He was a wonderful man, intelligent, capable, an expert bookkeeper. He was never one of my fishing or drinking companions, but he was totally trustworthy, the one man I could always depend on to do his job. As I kept pushing the company ahead, he sorted out everything in my wake. Like us all, of course, he grew older and eventually didn't have quite the same grip on everything and Gerry LaFortune was called on to handle more and more.

Gala was the first to notice something special about the young man. She was head of accounting when he joined the company and she worked very closely with him. When Mr. Tetu retired rather suddenly, Gerry stepped in and took over the books. As time went on, he stood out and, a little at a time, something about him got to me. Looking back, I haven't been able to pin down exactly what it was. There was nothing to tell me I might be able to plunge him into a type of work — selling and organizing — not related to accounting; yet both Gala and I sensed something in him.

I had a hunch he might be just the man to make Modern Cleaning Services work so I called him in one day and asked him if he would take it over. He turned me down! "I'm quite happy where I am, Mr. Pickering. Besides, there's no evidence I have the ability to do that sort of thing."

I am a determined man. OK then; I'm *stubborn!* I thought for a while, then said: "Gerry, I've started this new company and it's in trouble. As far as I know there are only two people in the world who can make it work. I'm one of them; and you're the other.

"Now I am *not* going to let Modern Cleaning Services fail, and to get it going is going to take eighteen months of hard slogging on the road. If you won't do it, I will. I'll do it and I *know* I can do it. But I'm seventy-five and it will kill me."

It was a great little speech. I looked him in the eye and waited. Finally he said: "You leave me no choice."

"I didn't intend to."

Then I rapidly learned something else about Gerry LaFortune: he wasn't going to be a yes man. He immediately insisted on setting up offices in a separate building so I wouldn't be looking over his shoulder all the time. Just once, some time later, I called in on him there without an appointment: he said he was too busy to see me! He worked marvelously hard, and he steered Modern back to my basic business principles of offering only top quality work at a fair price that always included a profit. He was no yes man, but he did agree with those principles.

I have always been convinced that a certain percentage of business people are more interested in quality than in cut prices. You can't have one organization that does all types of work — good, bad, and indifferent. We elected to offer good work only at a price in keeping with that quality. That was the policy which was so foreign to my two New Yorkers. Gerry went through all our contracts, canceled some, negotiated new prices on others, until he had the entire business back on a quality-only basis.

I always wanted to avoid shoddy work in all of my businesses. I remember during World War II we had a problem with turpentine. Good turpentine is made from resin exuded from the sapwood of pine and fir, and the best is colorless and transparent. We use only the best quality in our waxes. During the war they discovered they could make an inferior quality from stumps and fallen branches as well. One day our chemist said: "I think we can get away with using the cheaper stuff. We can camouflage it."

"Would it be as good?" I asked. "Would it turn out as good a product?"

"No, but I don't think most people will be able to tell the difference."

I bawled him out. "Never," I ordered, "suggest that we use a substitute to cheapen our products. We will *not* leave ourselves open like that. If you have something that's *better* I'll listen to you, even if it costs more. But if you have something that's cheaper and inferior, I won't." That's why today in Canada we have a reputation that's second to none. We acknowledge from the start that good quality maintenance costs a bit more, but that's all we supply.

By 1960 Gala had been president for about twelve years. I was seventy-nine but was still hanging in there as chief executive. The business, especially our contract cleaning, was growing very fast and becoming very complicated and starting to irritate Gala. She didn't really want to keep pace, and it reached the point where she thought she'd be happier out of it. She wanted to travel, among other things, while she was still young enough to enjoy it.

Next question: who should succeed her? There were only two candidates: my son-in-law, Gordon Pimm, who was working for Dustbane as vice-president of merchandising and manufacturing, and Gerry LaFortune who, in five years, had built Modern Cleaning Services into a five-million-dollar subsidiary. With relatives involved, it was an especially difficult decision.

Gordon Pimm is a truly excellent man and it was the luckiest thing in my life when June married him. He is a man for whom I have total respect. He and June met at McGill University where he was studying business administration. He

104 Introducing Lafortune

has a very logical mind and no weaknesses that I can put my finger on. However he does not have the *imagination* of a Gerry LaFortune.

I eventually reached a decision that satisfied myself and kept everybody happy. In addition to Dustbane and Modern, I have a family company, Michael's Industrial Equipment, which holds my stock in these companies and in various others. Michael's also supplies small dealers and jobbers who sell cleaning supplies and equipment under private label. (As they're competitors of our franchise dealers, Dustbane can't deal with them direct.) Michael's is an outlet for millions of dollars worth of products of my factory, and it also owns small cleaning companies. The management of Michael's fitted well with Pimm's business administration background. For the presidency of Dustbane, I selected Gerry LaFortune.

The relationship between the founder of a company and the man who takes over *can* be a difficult one. As I've said, Gerry is not a man you can order around; however he does agree with the principles on which my companies were founded. Having now watched him closely in action for twenty years, I realize that he is a management genius. If his health stands up, he will one day be head of a huge company; Dustbane and Modern together will be the General Motors of the cleaning business. He has the management ability to build a billion-dollar enterprise, provided he brings along managers beneath him to consolidate gains as he makes them.

Having acknowledged his superlative skills, I can make some negative comments without seeming condescending. (A man must have a few privileges at ninety-two!) On several occasions, as chairman of the board, I've had to decide whether to let Gerry have his head or to curb him. I always let him have his head. I have been determined not to destroy his imagination nor curb his courage; I wanted the full value of both in my business. I let him make mistakes, gambling that he would learn from them, and he did learn. Today he's almost super-cautious — by his own decision, not mine.

Gerry launched a contract cleaning business in Europe when I thought we had enough to do servicing the Canadian market. If I'd told him "No", he would have been frustrated and would never have believed that I was right to hold back. He went into it on a grand scale, then we couldn't hold it all together and had to pull back until we caught up with our domestic opportunities. That paid off. Today we have the European situation re-organized and consolidated and on a paying basis, and it's starting to take off. Our costly European "mistake" will convert into a very profitable venture.

In business your "mistakes" are often in the long run your most profitable ventures. They alert you, teach you the value of doing a thing right. But it's not easy for an old man to keep silent as he watches his younger successor make avoidable mistakes as part of his unavoidable learning process.

Gerry once tried to expand Dustbane's merchandising program. He wanted to enlist more "expert" salesmen than our usual people. He put new hot shots on salaries, which meant they could get money without working. I let him do that, too, although I was convinced I knew better. In our line of business, a highpowered salesman doesn't fit because you can't high-pressure a man who's buying cleaning supplies. He buys only what he *needs* and even that is almost against his will. This is not like buying something that he can resell at a profit. Ours is strictly an expense item, and no highpowered salesman is going to sell a man more than he needs. Our salesmen's relationship to customers is based upon service not sales power. In my early days, mind you, it was different. Then I was pioneering a product so I had to keep *selling*. Today we offer established products.

In every sense, Gerry LaFortune is a winner. The company today is three times the size it was when he took over and he personally holds so much stock he'll stay with the company for life. Many big U.S. companies have tried to buy us out simply to acquire his executive talents. One of the biggest soap companies in the world made a great offer, but when Gerry would only promise them a five-year management contract on his services, they stopped negotiating.

So now let's look again at that relationship between LaFortune and me, and its tensions, if any. If I'm recognized as a successful businessman today it's partly because Gerry has pushed me in front of him. It seems to me that, the bigger he gets the bigger I get, because I was the one who recognized his talent. *Wherever* he goes, and he's going a long long way, I go for the ride.

When I was young, people discovered things in me and encouraged me and gave me the confidence to go ahead. It's always other people who allow you to find things in yourself that you didn't know were there. My entire ambition was to drive a wagon until Gleason pushed me into sales. Similarly Gerry was happy to be a bookkeeper. He didn't know he could do a bigger job, just as I didn't know I could sell. I discovered I had a natural talent and went from the bottom to the top, and that's the sort of progress Gerry LaFortune has made since I gambled that he was the man, first to save Modern Cleaning Services and, later, to become president of Dustbane.

With Gerald D. LaFortune

Chapter 12

THE LORD ELGIN
Don't buck odds: undermine them

Your listing in *Who's Who* mentions many more business involvements than Dustbane, Modern Building Cleaning, and Michael's Industrial Equipment. It shows that one of your big interests for example, has been the hotel business.

In the last few years there has been a building boom in hotels in Canada, and people tend to take huge new hotels almost for granted. Back in 1940, however, the launching of a new hotel was seen as quite a significant community event. And 1940 was the year they built the Lord Elgin, one of the hotels you're associated with. *Was* it a big deal at the time, and how did you get involved?

OTTAWA NEEDED HOTELS. As the war brought in more and more business visitors, the capital found itself desperately short of decent hotel accommodation so I was appointed chairman of a Civic Industrial and Publicity sub-committee with the job of bringing a good hotel to the city. Through this work I met Jack Udd, one of the smartest men and best friends I ever knew, and it was he who introduced me to the hotel business.

From the start, the search for a hotel caused controversy. One newspaper declared that Alderman Pickering *knew* there was no chance of anyone building a decent hotel in Ottawa, and that I was only looking for cheap publicity. That editorial writer, whoever he was, made me more determined than ever.

The Lord Elgin

I remember very vividly the day I met Udd. Redverse Pratt, the paid manager of the Industrial and Publicity Committee, called me at about nine o'clock one morning to ask if I'd hustle up to his office. "There's a man here I want you to meet," he said. It was a gloomy fall morning as I walked around to Pratt's office which wasn't much more than a hole in the wall. There sat this tall, long-faced, guy with his overcoat and hat still on, looking about as gloomy as the morning. I learned in future weeks and years that Udd was never a fancy dresser; he always looked more like a farmer than a successful industrialist. Pratt introduced him. "This is Mr. Udd, the president of the Ford hotel chain."

Jack Udd lived in Rochester, New York. He had an engineering background but had moved into the hotel business. In 1928, he had built the Ford Hotel in Toronto, and later another in Montreal. There were Ford Hotels in the U.S., too, a chain of low-price dollar-a-day places that gave reasonably good value for the money. "Mr. Udd is interested in building a hotel in Ottawa," said Pratt.

I replied very quickly. "Ottawa is not interested in having a Ford Hotel."

Udd looked at me calmly. "The Ford Hotel Company has no intention of building its usual type of hotel in Ottawa. If we build here, it will be a modern high-quality hotel." That was more promising.

As we walked over to city hall together, he outlined three conditions under which he was prepared to get involved. We had to help him find a suitable site: we had to grant a low-cost fixed assessment for the hotel's first fifteen years; and local businessmen had to invest $250,000 in the project. I accepted the conditions and we promptly started looking for a site.

We ran into trouble straight away. Local landowners knew there was a hotel in the offing and, even though they knew the city desperately needed the new hotel, they all hiked their prices. I was disgusted.

For a couple of months we heard nothing but inflated prices. Then one day we stood looking across at an old gas station and some dilapidated buildings on government property at the north-west corner of Elgin and Laurier. I knew Udd was fed up and about ready to pull out, so I said to him grandly: *"There's* the site for your hotel!"

He gave me an exasperated look. "It'd be perfect. Of course. But why waste time dreaming! No private enterprise builds on government property."

"If you could get it, would you build there?"

"Of course. But it's not possible...."

I took Udd over to the office of Charlie Sutherland, the government's chief architect. "Charlie," I demanded, "what're the chances of building a hotel on that site on the corner of Elgin and Laurier?"

"Pick, they're one-in-a-million."

"Good enough!" Today the hotel is on that site. Since then I have always refused to believe that *anything's* impossible. A determined man can make a fair gamble out of one-in-a-million odds.

Admittedly I had to use some shenanigans. I knew, for example, that Prime Minister Mackenzie King longed to make Ottawa the most attractive capital in the world, so I was sure that the idea of cleaning up that dilapidated section would appeal to him. I didn't know King personally, but I knew his private secretary, Walter Turnbull. Redverse Pratt and I hatched a plan to use Turnbull to get a special picture before the Prime Minister. We made an architect's drawing of how the hotel would look on the site, then gave the newspapers the impression that getting permission to build there was almost a foregone conclusion. Udd feared our complicated scheme would backfire and that then he would have to take responsibility for it, but he went along. Just as we guessed would happen, the picture appeared on the front page of the newspapers and we rushed one to Walter Turnbull who placed it fair in the center of the Prime Minister's desk. We heard later from Turnbull that, when the "Old Man" came in, even though those were the busiest hours of the war, he spent a full half-hour looking at that picture and daydreaming. The stage was set. Now I called my friend Bill Fraser.

William Alexander Fraser was five years younger than me. He had grown up in Trenton, which is mid-town Ontario, and that was the heart of political power in those days. He had a sizeable farm, directed a number of companies, and had been mayor of Trenton from 1924 to 1930 and a Liberal MP for five years. Now he was party Whip, a very powerful man, and King used him as his right hand. I asked: "Will you come over to my office tomorrow morning at nine o'clock, Bill?"

He would. Then I called Udd and asked him for nine the next morning too.

Right on time they both walked in and I introduced them. I told Fraser: "I want that site. I want a lease so we can build."

"You want that hotel badly, don't you Pick?"

"More than I ever wanted anything in my life."

He thought for a moment. Then Fraser, who was about five-foot-four,

The Lord Elgin

looked up at Udd who was six-feet-four and said: "Come on, you big bastard. Come with me." They headed for the Houses of Parliament, and from that day on everything progressed beautifully. Udd leased that corner property for ninety-nine years at a low rental. The government gave us a fair deal because it wanted a hotel as much as we did.

As government land, it had been paying no taxes and never would pay any if Udd didn't build there. Although the hotel was to cost $925,000, he wanted a $308,000 valuation for the first fifteen years. Similar deals had been made in other cities wanting to attract hotels but, when I asked council to approve the deal, they ganged up on me. That old Ottawa caution was clogging progress again. They complained that, by taxing at only one-third the building's value, the city would lose two-thirds of its revenue. I argued that they were wrong, that this way they would get a third — plus a desperately needed hotel — whereas otherwise they'd get nothing.

My logic had little effect on them. There was all sorts of maneuvering and numerous votes before, in April 1940, the special assessment was finally approved — by fourteen votes to thirteen.

I had now met two of Udd's three conditions. The third was my promise that local people would put up a quarter-million dollars. Before making that commitment in the first place, I had called a meeting of businessmen and put it to them. "Jack Udd will build a hotel," I explained, "if you fellows will subscribe to a quarter-million dollars' worth of bonds."

"Sure," they all said. "Sure. We'll subscribe." But I knew those men, they were all my associates in business or politics, and I knew darned well most would probably run out on me. And they did. When it came time to collect their money they always had a million excuses. I was disgusted, and so was Udd. However he was still sold on *me*. "Don't worry too much about it, Pick," he said. "I'll saw off a hundred thousand with the contractor and the people selling us supplies. I'll make *them* take $100,000 in bonds. That will reduce your problem to $150,000."

It was a fair compromise, but I still had to raise $150,000. One day I asked him: "Would you accept $150,000 from Canadian Pacific Railways?"

"That won't work," he said. "CPR has an agreement with Canadian National not to build a hotel in Ottawa."

"I didn't *ask* you that. I asked if CPR money would be acceptable."

"Of course. But you can't get it."

Three weeks later he invited me to keep him company on a trip to

Montreal. While he went about his business there, I telephoned Sir Edward Beatty, president of CPR.

Edward Wentworth Beatty, G.B.E., K.C., LL.D. D.C.L., was a big man in Canadian business. He had been president of Canadian Pacific for twenty years and was also busy at this time helping the war effort by setting up the Transatlantic Air Ferry service. His two great loves were the railroad, and McGill University of which he was Chancellor. He was a defiant individualist and a man of dominating personality. However, I was a Controller. That gave me enough prestige to get an appointment and at two o'clock I walked into his office. I didn't beat about the bush. "I'm here to ask for something that you will immediately tell me is impossible. I'm going to ask anyway. . . ."

I explained the situation. Then I said: "If CP gives me my $150,000, it will get all the freight for all the material coming to that hotel. If not, it will only get half the freight. It's city policy to share freight between Canadian National and Canadian Pacific but, if we have a reason to justify it, we can give you all the new hotel's business."

He scratched his jaw. He stared out the window. He fiddled with the ornaments on his desk. And I kept very quiet. After my opening pitch I said hardly a word. For a long, long time he thought out loud. "We do have that agreement about not building a hotel in Ottawa," he murmured. "But there are ways around that . . . . . "

I knew there were ways around it. There always are. The CP empire controls rich trust companies, for example. There were plenty of ways to get that money to us. Finally he said: "We'll see what can be done." I got the $150,000.

His three conditions now met, Udd started building the hotel. From the start, Mackenzie King took a personal interest. Have you noticed the fancy roof on the Lord Elgin? It's like the roof on Parliament buildings. King wanted that. It cost about $150,000 extra.

King wanted stone and not brick. Udd compromised and agreed to use stone at both ends and on the front, but he'd put brick in the back. When I was on the construction side one day, I found King's own architect muttering to himself: "The Old Man is sorry, the Old Man is sorry." Sorry about what, I asked. "Sorry he agreed that Mr. Udd could use brick in the back." Just then Udd walked up so I told him the Prime Minister was upset about the brick. Udd asked: "Is that the only thing your 'Old Man' is upset about? Then go tell him I'll put stone in the back too."

King himself virtually designed the pillars in front of the hotel then, after they went up, he decided they were too big to blend with the building. He acknowledged to Udd that it was too bad he'd made that mistake. "Mr. Prime Minister," said Udd, "don't worry about it. We'll reduce them in size. However we'll have to wait until the war's over, because it's too hard right now to get workmen and material." And when the war was over, King called Udd and said: "Don't forget your promise to fix those pillars!" It must have cost Udd $15,000 to cut them down to size.

And so the Lord Elgin was built and King happily agreed to lay the cornerstone. On the day of the ceremony, however, the Germans invaded Paris and it seemed that Britain might not survive. It was the darkest day of the war. On the spur of the moment I had a scroll created to put in the cornerstone along with the usual coins and the day's newspapers with their sad headlines. The scroll declared: "We who are living today have faith that there'll always be an England and that democracy will prevail." Mackenzie King, the mayor, Udd, I, all the attending dignitaries, signed it and it's in that cornerstone now. Seventy-five or eighty years in the future, when they tear the Lord Elgin down, someone will discover that scroll and will see that, on the darkest day of the war, we all went on the record and confidently said: "We shall survive."

Jack Udd grew very fond of Canada, and he and I developed a great personal friendship because I was one of the first politicians he had met who wasn't on the make. I introduced him to prominent people and this lanky American appealed to them all. Gradually he developed more business interests here than in the United States, and in 1945 he moved his headquarters and home to Brockville, Ontario. Eventually he became a Canadian citizen.

When I pulled out of city politics, he invited me to join the board of the Lord Elgin. And *that,* my friend, is how I got into the hotel business.

Chapter 13

MORE TIME IN HOTELS

It seems you can't win them all

To any outsider the hotel business seems a bit romantic. We've all read of the jolly "mine hosts" of Dickensian times. Today diplomats, film stars, millionaires, tycoons, lovers and haters pass in and out of the big hotels and can expect their demands for good food, exotic drinks, respectful service all to be met.

How active a hotel man were you? Did you just sit in on directors' meetings, or did you dig deeply into the business? Were you interested in financial aspects alone, or were you also involved in promotion, hospitality, and the temperament of short-order chefs?

HOTELS ARE CERTAINLY FASCINATING. At first, however, I was involved only at board level. Udd invited me onto the board of the full North American chain, and that was a very fine board to be part of. It included a vice-president of the First National Bank of New York, officers of the Marine Trust Company, and many other prominent business people. Later Udd sold the chain to Sheraton Hotels under a plan which let him nominate three directors to the Sheraton board. I was one of his three and met people on that board who were even more prominent. It was a broadening experience for the boy from East Blackstone.

Long after my term on the Sheraton board, Udd called me to say that the chain needed a million dollars in cash and were willing to sell the Lord Elgin to get it. "If you can raise $500,000 in Ottawa," said Udd, "I can raise the

118   *More time in hotels*

other half-million in Montreal, and we can buy back our old hotel." A few intimate friends and I joined with the Montreal group and I became one of the largest stock holders in the Lord Elgin.

Later we sold the hotel to a New York chain, but retained the general mortgage bonds, and I continued to manage the place through The National Management Company which Udd had formed earlier and which I had taken over. I ran the hotel in that way for about twelve years for various New Yorkers who kicked it around and bought and resold it. That was a very disagreeable experience. Those New York businessmen, as I've said before, have a different philosophy and different values to ours. They seem to *enjoy* a vicious way of doing business; there's almost a strange good-palship in their attempts to cut each other's throat. I'd had my business training in Boston and New York so I was equipped to deal with them, but I still found it disagreeable. They wanted to take everything they could out of the hotel whereas I wanted to keep the place up and take a pride in it. It was an eternal battle.

The last of the New York owners, Arthur Cohen, won the hotel when its owners defaulted on a loan and he foreclosed. I promptly flew to New York to see him. He was a young fellow of about forty-three, a big operator who always traveled by private jet and used a helicopter to get to and from his home outside New York City. While I was there, a battery of phones kept ringing, and there were quick conversations about fifteen million dollars, eighteen million dollars.

Between calls, I told him that I hadn't come down to argue about anything but just to meet him. I think he'd recently seen "My Fair Lady" because he called me "Colonel Pickering". He didn't know one thing about the Lord Elgin and admitted that he didn't like hotel operations. Nor did he like having a foreign investment. "Why don't you come up and see your property?" I asked. "Have you ever been to Ottawa?"

"Where's Ottawa?" he demanded. "Have they got an airport there?" Somewhat reluctantly he agreed to come and told his secretary to order his plane for a certain day. On that day he and his fourteen-year-old daughter flew up in a jet that could have brought ten people. He went straight to the hotel and phoned me, and I came in to show him around, but he was very impatient and keen to get back to New York. As I drove out to the airport with him, he said: "Your group holds the general mortgage bonds. What do they amount to?"

"A million six."

"What if we change places? I'll take over your bonds and you take over the hotel."

"That's not a bad idea. But I don't think your equity is equal to ours. However, I'll get in touch."

I made an appointment to meet him in New York and took along my lawyer and my financial expert. As we drove into Manhattan, I said to them: "You two just keep quiet and listen. You're about to hear a New York Jew and a New England Yankee do a little horsetrading."

Cohen and I immediately started to fence over whether his equity in the hotel was worth as much as our $1,600,000. I said I didn't really want to make a deal, and he said he really didn't want to make one either. We kept on in that way until I eventually made him an offer: $1,100,000. He said he was shocked. "Do you know what your offer means? The hotel makes that amount in *profit* in ten years! You will buy my equity out of profits and get the hotel for nothing! No deal!"

My lawyer and my financial man bit their tongues, but looked at me as if to say: "Now what, smart Yankee?" I stood up. "Mr. Cohen, it's been a good day's work. I've accomplished everything I expected to when I came here. I'm going back to Ottawa as happy as a lark."

"What do you mean! What did you accomplish? We haven't made a deal."

"I didn't *expect* to make a deal. I've had the management of that hotel for the past twelve years and, under the people who owned it, it has been a very disagreeable experience. Now it's in the hands of a man I can do business with. You own the hotel and I'll manage it, and we'll all be happy together." I turned for the door.

"Alright," he capitulated. "You've got a deal."

I'd called his bluff. I knew he didn't want that hotel, and I knew he didn't want a foreign investment. And *that's* how I bought the Lord Elgin. I took two close friends in with me but kept sixty-five percent of the stock for myself.

Since then I've had various dealings with Arthur Cohen and it has been a most pleasurable business relationship. Cohen's word is good on everything. I think he enjoys me as a novelty. He can't quite believe that a man of ninety can dicker with him at his own level. Last time I visited him in New York he took me from office to office, showing me off to his people.

One December a couple of years ago I was in Ottawa for a directors'

120 *More time in hotels*

meeting when Cohen and his wife called from the hotel. They were passing through on a skiing trip. When he heard that I was spending every winter in Florida, he said: "I have a real estate development down there, Colonel. Take a look at it, then 'phone me and let me know what you think of it."

"My opinion of real estate is not worth anything."

"Go and see it anyway. I'll phone my manager and tell him you're coming." When I got back to Miami, I looked his "development" over. It is a $600-million community and he's in partnership on it with Ari Onassis. I immediately bought a condominium apartment there; it is now my winter home.

Almost all my dealings on the Lord Elgin were satisfying. I wish I could say the same thing about my other major involvement in the hotel business. That was a disaster from the start.

Jack Udd was a big operator. He was personally worth about forty million dollars and he also had access to plenty of money. For years it seemed that he could do no wrong in business. He always gave me a piece of his mining schemes, even though I knew nothing about them. I'd keep the stock a while then sell it and usually make a dollar. Then he and Harry Wheal, who owned Standard Electric, promoted a new hotel for Toronto. They planned to call it: The Lord Simcoe.

Simcoe was the first Lieutenant-Governor of Upper Canada, which is now Ontario, and he was never a Lord. I guess Udd and Wheal elevated him to the peerage to give the hotel a little more class and to link it with Ottawa's Lord Elgin. Maybe that minor fiddle with the truth should have put me off straight away. I never did especially like the deal but I went along with it because Udd almost never made business mistakes. I put in $100,000 as an initial investment.

Prominent people were involved. Fred Gardiner, later known as "Big Daddy" when he became first chairman of Metropolitan Toronto, was a director. Abe Bronfman of Seagram's put in nearly a half-million dollars. Howard Webster, owner of the Globe & Mail, had a big investment. Sherman Hotels of Chicago came in too.

Sherman wanted to start a high-class restaurant in Toronto like their famous Pump Room in Chicago and they thought the Lord Simcoe would be a good setting. Big mistake! The Lord Simcoe, like the Lord Elgin, was aimed at the "commercial" trade, designed and built for people who wanted good economy. It was no luxury hotel, no place for a luxury restaurant. I'd eaten in the Chicago Pump Room once and knew that, with all those waiters hanging around, it was certainly not the sort of place I'd seek out. When the Sherman people convinced the board that a Pump Room would be good for the Simcoe, I was the only one who questioned the decision. Udd at the time was too busy trying to save one of his mining projects to give the hotel his full attention.

Basically, hotels sell space and Udd's policy, which had always been very successful, was to provide small rooms at a comparatively low cost. The Lord Elgin has been consistently profitable over the years, and its earning power per square foot is higher than that of all the more expensive hotels. That high-priced Pump Room at the Lord Simcoe discouraged the very clientele the hotel needed to attract.

Everything went against the place and the rumor mill worked overtime. Once, when I told a cab-driver to take me to the Lord Simcoe, he warned me: "Stay away from that place. It's just a clip joint. You're not welcome in the Pump Room unless you spend fifty dollars!" Someone else once tried to tell me that the rooms are so small you have to put one foot on the bathtap to sit on the toilet.

I spent about a year trying to get the Lord Simcoe on the rails and working with me was John Ostiguy, Jack Udd's personal assistant, who later became secretary of Dustbane. We lived in adjoining rooms at the hotel, went down to breakfast together every morning at seven, then put in a long day's work. Ostiguy tells friends we were once moving along the line carrying our trays in the hotel cafeteria when I asked him: "See anything funny about that peach pie?" He said it looked fine to him. I pointed out: "It should be over there in the twenty-cent section, not here with the fifteen-cent stuff!" The Lord Simcoe needed every nickel it could get.

Relentlessly the hotel's troubles increased and disagreements on the board grew fiercer. Howard Webster was a very difficult man. He'd inherited wealth and he has made a lot of money on his own too, and he thought he knew all the answers. He wanted the Sheraton chain to run the hotel instead of my National Management. When he persisted, Jack Udd and I decided to get rid of him and made a deal to buy him out. Udd, Bill Fraser, and I would buy his shares and later we'd get another friend of ours William Zeckendorf Jr. in on the deal too. I put up $300,000 in securities and $100,000 in cash, and Udd put up $600,000 in securities and $300,000 in cash. Zeckendorf and

Fraser were to come in with their share later to pay the further instalments to complete our deal.

Before those instalments were paid, however, everything changed. Udd died; Fraser died; Zeckendorf went broke, and I found myself alone. Either I had to find all the rest of the money myself or write off the $400,000 I'd already invested. I went to Gerry LaFortune, who was running Modern Building Cleaning, and to Gala, who was president of Dustbane, and told them: "I think I can save this investment, if I form a holding company and merge Dustbane with the hotel." They were strongly against the idea.

I thought it all over very carefully. I was seventy-six, and whatever I started they would have to finish. That hardly seemed fair to them when they were so against it. I decided to forfeit. Webster took all the collateral that Udd and I had put up; in total about a million dollars. *That* was my association with the Lord Simcoe!

These days, I think, the Lord Simcoe is finally making some money, but there's a branch of the Canadian Imperial Bank of Commerce where the Pump Room used to be. I couldn't care less: when the furor was all over I bundled up the last few shares I owned in the company and gave them to our housekeeper.

Chapter 14

NEW ENTERPRISE
Hopefully, a $100 - million sideline

We've talked about Dustbane, and we've talked about Modern, and about Michael's and about your hotel interests. That's a lot of enterprises to launch in one lifetime. But apparently you're still not prepared to sit back and enjoy the Florida sunshine in winter and the Ottawa sunshine in summer. Didn't you recently launch an entirely new operation?

I'VE A NEW AMERICAN COMPANY. At ninety-one I launched a U.S. business that has more exciting short-term and long-term prospects than anything I've touched before. My son-in-law, Gordon Pimm, is heading it up and a grandson is also involved. The other day when I was explaining to them how fast their new company will grow, Pimm suddenly said: "You're amazing! Here you are just starting something, and already in your mind you've got it listed on the New York Stock Exchange." Perhaps I shouldn't be so cocksure about how it will grow but I *know* it will be a reality. You wait and watch and see. I think I'll wait and watch and see it myself, too, if I can.

My grandson got involved after he came to Canada from Florida a few years ago to learn the contract cleaning business. He spent about two years in Modern, then moved back to Georgia because he wanted to start a company of his own. He asked his mother to back him but I knew that the money he was asking her for was only a drop in the bucket of what he would need, and he had no idea what he was getting into. I called him. "I'll finance you in Florida," I said, "providing you stick to a plan I've worked out." The plan I then outlined to him will eventually build the largest contract cleaning company in the United States. Already we're moving, and we're moving fast. We have five units working in Florida which are proving my theory.

We have set up, essentially, a franchise business that overcomes the greatest difficulty in contract cleaning, which is finding and keeping reliable employees who can supervise the work. Contract cleaners have to deliver service and quality, and they have to take all the headaches away from building management. For each big building, the contract cleaner provides a supervisor. If this man neglects his job and doesn't stay on top of it twenty-four hours a day, you quickly have a dirty building and an angry client. When a building is not clean every morning you soon lose your contract and your reputation.

In this new American setup, when a young man shows up who is really keen on establishing himself, we tell him: "You have assets that we lack: youth, ability, enthusiasm. We have assets you lack: working capital, business experience. We will merge your assets with ours. If you will carry out our plan, we will set you up in business." We then subtract from his gross revenues fifteen percent to cover financing, accounting, bookkeeping and sales. He draws about $750 a month and in addition receives a bonus in common shares in the parent company, but he may not deviate from our policy. We own the company because we own the preferred shares which we can convert into common anytime we want. We earmark about eight percent in addition for our profit, and he takes the balance. We can be satisfied with about eight percent because eventually it will be on a huge volume.

My plan guarantees that each young man will be more serious in seeing that his customers are serviced properly because it's *his* business. There is a direct relationship between the customers and the people who control the quality. He may do some of the cleaning himself or he may hire others to do it all. No franchise will be very big because we control the size. The Toronto-Dominion Centre, for example, is about a hundred thousand dollar a month contract. Under a franchise system that would be all one fellow could handle.

It all revolves around putting these young men in a position where they can make profits and have a certain independence. If they stand out, they will get bigger contracts because we'll have learned we can trust them. As they take a percentage of their profits in common shares in the parent company they will all have a stake in its well-being. The young men we're after are not the businessmen type but the enthusiastic workers who want to get out of the rank and file.

Finding that type of young man is the key to the contract cleaning business. There's an abundance of labor around to do the actual cleaning. A lot of women are happy to go out from seven to eleven o'clock at night to pick up six or eight dollars. We can maintain a pool of that type of worker. But at the supervisory level, it gets more difficult every day to find competent people. To keep them, you have to cut them in on the profits.

This U.S. venture will take a lot of financing. In Canada alone our payroll is about a million-and-a-half a month, and there's a forty-five or fifty day timelag before customers pay you. These young fellows can't carry that sort of debt, but I can. So far we've financed the U.S. company from our own resources but there's always credit available when we want it. When I talked to the president of a Miami bank that's affiliated with a trust company I'm associated with, he simply said: "You can have all the financing you need." A young man can't get that sort of treatment. That's what I mean about pooling resources.

The U.S. business will reach $100-million a year by 1985. Easily. Just look at the scope of it! In Canada we have a Post Office contract that pays $500,000 a year, hospitals that run to $400,000 a year. With this new franchising idea to overcome the supervisor difficulties, we can do $100-million-a-year in the U.S. and have no inventory because essentially all we need is labor, and you only pay labor when you use it. You don't have to store it in warehouses. I can hardly wait to see it all come true — New York Stock Exchange listing and all!

Chapter 15

FRIENDS AT THE TOP
It's still mostly a man's world

A fascinating aspect of your life is that you have seen North American society from both ends. As a teenager you experienced the seamy side yet, even there, you found people who were kind to a boy on his own in the world. For the last half-century, you have worked and played at the other end — with the rich and prominent, with politicians, promoters, developers, officials, social leaders, with men and women whose names were often in headlines. You met them both through business and through your political and public service career.

Some people imagine that the greatest reward of success is money, but surely there is an equal satisfaction in hobnobbing with successful, effective, *involved* people.

Tell us about some of them.

IMPORTANT PEOPLE. I daresay there were lots of them. I met General Eisenhower before he became president. I was introduced to King George and Queen Elizabeth (she whispered to him that his hat was not straight). I met Lindbergh, the aviator. I even "met" Teddy Roosevelt back in the days when I was shoveling potatoes out of a freight car for Gleason. (Roosevelt's private train was backed up at a siding next to ours. When he climbed out onto the platform a few of us were able to small talk with him. He was the first president I ever voted for.) Despite my lack of education, I never felt uncomfortable or at a disadvantage with such people. I think that was because I didn't pretend to be something I wasn't.

132 *Friends at the top*

I had a few conversations with Viscount Alexander when he was Governor-General. When I dreamed up the idea that everyone should donate one day's income to the United Nations appeal for children, he agreed to make the first contribution. The press photographers were all there because the aim was to get publicity for the cause. As Alexander handed me his cheque the press crowded in to see how much it was for. He grinned and handed it to me upside down; and I folded it and put it away. Of course I looked later to see what the amount was but I didn't reveal it, and now I've forgotten. The next time I saw him was when he invested me with the O.B.E.

When Fiorello La Guardia, the mayor of New York, visited Ottawa he and I talked for a long time about how our two city governments handle things. Later he invited mayor Stanley Lewis, one other alderman, and me to New York as guests of the city. We stayed five days at the Waldorf Astoria, with private detectives looking after us around the clock. City cars were waiting for us whenever we wanted them, and all the night life of New York was free. When one of those detectives led us into a nightclub *everything* was laid on. We saw the sights and met prominent citizens and kept going night and day. One police car drove me down through the heart of Manhattan with its siren wailing, and at every intersection a traffic cop waved us through. Everyone stared at the guy in the back seat wondering if he were the king of Denmark, or a film star. It was far different from an earlier trip I had made down Third Avenue.

In Ottawa, of course, I had many business and political contacts, and every Wednesday night throughout the war a number of us sat down for the weekly "fish dinner". Senator McLean, Administrator of Fishery Products, flew fresh fish in from British Columbia or the Maritimes every week and a dozen top men from the Liberal Party settled in to a private suite for food, drink, talk, gossip, and laughs. At one time or another all the key government people let their hair down at these dinners. They needed a chance to relax because government operations were very tense during the war.

In the four-and-a-half years of fish dinners I overheard many things that people outside the caucus were not supposed to hear. The debate on conscription was practically *settled* in that room. No one present ever repeated anything outside.

One evening McLean brought in a barrel of paper-thin oysters from a government experimental bed in Prince Edward Island. We had a competition to see who could eat the most and I won by swallowing eighteen-dozen-

and-three. Someone took the knife we all used and one of the shells and made a "trophy" with a silver plaque to note the names of contestants.

Frequently present was Donald Gordon, who'd been deputy governor of the Bank of Canada and was now chairman of the Wartime Prices and Trade Board, a very powerful, responsible, exhausting position. As a temporary civil servant he could be criticized in the House of Commons but could not stand up and fight back except through his minister. He came to a fish dinner one night when he'd just had a horrible going-over in the House. He was always a two-fisted drinker, and that night he drank more than usual until, big six-foot-four man that he was, he broke down and cried. "I'm going to resign," he mumbled. "I can't *take* that abuse." Senator Fraser, a close friend of Gordon's, was an ex-navy man with a big powerful chest but was only about five-feet-four. He glared up at his friend who was twelve inches taller than him and bellowed: "Shake yourself out of that you big stiff." He just gave him blazes, and Gordon snapped right out of it.

I was on a first-name basis with C.D. Howe, the brilliant American who converted Canada's industry into an effective war machine. That friendship proved handy when Jack Udd wanted to build a hotel in Montreal because hotels weren't on the priority list for steel. Udd and I went to see Howe in his office. He was in his shirt sleeves with his feet on the desk and, although he'd never met with Udd, he said immediately: "You're here to get steel for that hotel." We nodded. He flicked across to us the official list of "prohibited uses". Hotels were near the top.

"I've seen *that* before," I said. "We didn't walk all the way up Parliament Hill to look at some damned list." Howe threw it into a drawer, and then scowled at us for a while. "Oh Hell," he said finally. "Go on and build your damn' hotel. War or no war, it's sadly needed." And that's how Udd built The Laurentian.

It was after the war that I got to know William Zeckendorf, the great developer of Place Ville Marie and many other huge projects. In his period of expansion he negotiated to buy the Ford Hotel chain and Jack Udd invited me to join the two of them on a fishing trip while they discussed it. Udd flew his own plane to a fishing club a hundred miles north of Ottawa, and the three of us strolled into camp. When Zeckendorf spied a deck of cards on the dining room table, he suggested: "Cut the cards with you, Pick?"

"OK."

"How much?"

"Oh, a thousand dollars."

"Fine," he agreed, and grabbed the deck.

"No, no, no," I said quickly. "Better make that ten cents."

"OK." He said it just as if there were no difference between the two. Zeckendorf and Udd and I then cut cards together for an hour. He won fifty cents and was delighted.

Bill Zeckendorf is a fine man. He started his business career in New York, where some very wealthy people took a fancy to him and backed him. Every entrepreneur wants quick growth but he had a different way of achieving it. He borrowed money to buy property then paid cash for it, charging the fierce interest rates he was paying against the purchase price. He'd borrow twenty million dollars on short-term at eighteen percent, pay cash for a property, find a buyer, make a capital gain, and get out fast. The scheme worked fine as long as the real estate market kept booming; but then the market went flat, and Zeckendorf was caught and couldn't sell, and they closed in on him.

I saw him every time I visited New York and he was always spectacular. When he took me to a championship fight we had front-row seats that must have cost $150 each. Once I was his guest at the Commodore Hotel which he owned. He picked me up at the airport in a chauffeured limousine, then put me into a suite — three bedrooms, sitting room, dining room — that had been built for President Eisenhower. I stood at the hotel window that night and looked down at the river and saw the very place where, so many years ago, I had sneaked in under the tarpaulin on a scow to get out of the rain.

Once in New York I noticed a newspaper picture of Zeckendorf handing over a cheque for fifty million dollars to the owners of the Chrysler building which he had just bought. I decided I shouldn't bother him as he had such a big deal underway. A few days later in Ottawa, one of my daughters reported: "We had a nice time in New York, thanks to your Mr. Zeckendorf". On that very day she had called Zeckendorf to see if he could get her some Broadway tickets. "Certainly I can," he said, "but you'll have to come up here to get them so that I can meet you." That afternoon he spent a leisurely, courteous hour showing them around his fantastic windowless offices that were designed by a Chinese architect. Two or three times he dodged back into his private office for a moment. That was how he concluded a $50-million transaction.

When he bought Sherman hotels, he picked up a share of my National

Management Company. I rushed to New York because his policy was to buy and sell quickly. As I walked into his fancy office, he said: "Have you got any money?"

"What sort of money?"

"Ten thousand dollars."

"Sure."

On the spot he sold me some stock in Webb & Knapp, his Canadian subsidiary. He didn't even ask me if I *wanted* it. I was delighted to get off the hook for a mere $10,000. I was scared he would ask me for a couple of million. (I kept that stock even after Zeckendorf got into trouble. It was converted into shares of Trizec Corporation and is today worth a certain amount.)

"Bill," I said, "along with the assets of Sherman Hotels you got a piece of National Management Company."

"I did? I didn't know that."

"That means you're in partnership with me." He grinned at that. I continued: "I figure the devil you know is better than the devil you don't, so I want you to hang on to that National Management interest and not sell it with the rest of the property."

"What do you want me to do with it? Give it to you?"

"Just keep it personally."

Years after that, just before he went broke, he was desperate for cash and called me. "Make me an offer for that National Management interest," he demanded.

I made him an offer. He asked: "Is that what it's worth?"

"Yes."

"If you say so, it's a deal."

That was the way he made deals. His word was always solid.

Every year he came to Quebec to fish. One day, after a long afternoon in the boat together, I asked: "Want to get back to camp?" He nodded. He was in the bow of the boat and I was in the stern, so I turned, adjusted the motor then, hauled on the starter. As the boat took off I heard a shout and a splash and turned to see big Bill Zeckendorf floundering in the lake like a 220-pound seal. Just as I started the boat, he had stood up to relieve himself.

I never learned whether he came out of his financial collapse with a bankroll. I've seen him since and he's subdued, but not depressed. I don't think he could ever be depressed.

With Fiorello La Guardia, (centre) mayor of New York

Chapter 16

DRINKING DAYS

Fun until his cup ran over

You've referred to a number of these successful, hard-working men as "two-fisted drinkers", which raises interesting points. Our society in some ways seems to deny the amount of drinking done by almost all men at almost all levels. Eighty-five percent of Canadian men drink an average of two gallons of alcohol a year, and that's a lot of drinking! Thirty-three percent of what they drink is liquor, ten percent is wine, and fifty-seven percent is beer. Some of that drinking is the restrained single sherry or martini before dinner; but plenty is of the other variety, the gutsy, boisterous business of tying one on with your friends.

I've often wondered why so many of us drink so much. The Ontario Alcoholism and Drug Addiction Research Foundation figures that drinking nine ounces of whisky or six bottles of beer every day can be harmful and that, by those standards, 700,000 Canadians drink enough to endanger their health.

Yet drinking doesn't *necessarily* interfere with work performance. Your experience among highly successful and creative people proves that heavy drinking is by no means confined to failures. The successful drink just as much as the unsuccessful.

Did you ever find that drinking — your own or other people's — was a handicap in business or politics?

DRINKING IS NO HANDICAP. In business it can be just the reverse. Drinking mellows people so that you can get closer to them. It rounds off the rough edges. Among all my business associates, George Green was the only man who suffered seriously from it. Provided they can handle it properly, liquor can help two businessmen get closer together faster and reach a better understanding than they could without it. Almost all people can handle it properly and just the smallest percentage — only one in twenty-five on a national average — gets into difficulties.

I was always a bit wary with liquor. I drank a lot but I never made the mistake of thinking I was its boss. I recognized it as a powerful factor to be careful of. I never liked the *taste* of the stuff much, but I liked its effect. I was a "shot drinker". When the bartender poured it, I drank it straight off.

Throughout my business career I had great party nights, but I'd always be up and out as fresh as a daisy again the next morning. I didn't get hangovers. I was too busy to drink before six o'clock at night.

As I got into my seventies and had more spare time, drinking became more of a factor and I dropped my rule of waiting until six o'clock. If I was at home, I'd take a drink in the morning to keep me going for a while, and then take another. In that way, you can get yourself into a very comfortable state, quite happy and relaxed. But liquor plays tricks on you and I found I was taking more of it all the time. At first a couple of drinks have a certain effect, then it takes three to do the same job. Eventually, no matter how much you drink, you don't get the same reaction — but you keep on trying, and it's that attempt to recapture the original thrill that leads so many people to alcoholism.

Eventually I was drinking a bottle of Hennessy's brandy a day. I knew it was a fairly dangerous quantity but that didn't worry me too much. I was into my seventies, my business was in good hands, my family was raised and secure; my job was done. If I was shortening my life I didn't care. But then one day I received a letter from a very dear, old friend who said: "Do you realize how much your drinking is hurting the people who love you?" I was totally surprised and her letter got me thinking, because I have always claimed that the only real sin is to hurt other people.

I started wondering: who's running your life? Why is some other power doing it? I decided that, while I still had power to be boss, I had better assert that power. I took all my liquor and packed it in the closet, and I've never been near it since. I didn't tell myself that I'd never take another drink. I just said I wouldn't take one until I really *wanted* it and since then I've never *really* wanted one. And thus, after more than a half-century of great parties

Drinking days 141

and roaring sociability, my drinking days ended quite peacefully and painlessly.

But, aah, the parties we had!

In my early days of traveling and selling, all salesmen, no matter how hard they worked, had time on their hands and, after a day's work in a strange town, someone would always say: "Let's go to the bar and have a beer." We were wandering men in cold hotels away from our families. We did it for fellowship. That's how it started.

Nearly all those top-notch Ottawa men were two-fisted drinkers. That regular "fish dinner" evening was established to help them unwind, and that meant *heavy* drinking. Paul Martin, C.D. Howe, Arthur Slaght were all good drinkers. But they could *handle* it. I never saw anyone there who didn't have his faculties about him.

Jack Udd was another big drinker. Sometimes when we went fishing we'd sit by a creek somewhere and uncap a twenty-six-ouncer and forget the fish until we had finished the bottle. Time and again I tried to drink him under the table, but I never succeeded. I'd put myself away first.

One great drinking crony was Pete Lynch, an Irishman with a leprechaun's humor, who worked for me in Toronto. When I went down there, he and I would work hard all day, then take a forty-ounce bottle of Seagram's to my room in the King Edward Hotel, and drink the whole bottle. One night after we'd done that, we came out of the King Eddie and saw an old taxicab standing there, with two passengers but no driver. I put my head in the window and asked: "Where's your driver?"

"We don't know, he's disappeared."

"Then *I'll* drive you!" Pete and I piled into the front seat and off we went.

"Peter," I ordered after a while, "collect the fares!"

"From whom?"

"From our passengers, of course."

"We have no passengers. Those two fellows left this cab just as fast as we got in!"

We came to a construction site with a red warning light. "Peter," I ordered, "get the red light. They'll think we're the fire department." Off we went again, with Pete Lynch waving the light out the window. After a couple of blocks we accidentally arrived back at the King Eddie to find a fellow waving his arms in the middle of the street. I stopped. "What do you want?"

"I want my cab! This is *mine* and you stole it!"

"Can you drive it?"

"Of course I can drive it. It's *my* cab!"

"Well get in then and drive it." Before he exploded with fury I handed him a ten-dollar bill, which helped him see that it was all quite funny.

Pete and I were always cutting up. In February 1940 I was elected a director of the Ottawa Football Club and remained one for the next twenty-six years. I followed the Rough Riders whenever they went to Toronto and, as Pete had once played football, we always went to the game together. On football days we broke our no-drinks-before-six rule and shared our friendly forty-ouncer in the *middle* of the day. Then we'd hurry through our business, and head for the game.

One evening Pete parked the company car at a gas station across the street from Maple Leaf Stadium. Just before the game finished, I went down to the men's room, then got lost in all those hallways under the grandstand. The game came to an end, everyone shuffled out, and I was still lost. When I finally found the exit everybody was gone. Including Pete. And the car.

"The beggar," I thought. "He's left me!" I wandered around, fuzzily trying to think what to do, when suddenly I saw a car sitting empty with a key in the ignition. "Since *our* car has gone," I thought, "I'll obviously have to take this one." It seemed quite a reasonable proposition. I suppose I figured that, if I was picked up, I would get out of it with some story or other. The police would have to know a man in my position wouldn't *steal* a car. "They'll see the funny side of it," I thought confidently. Luckily, I didn't have to check that theory out because I drove to the King Edward without being stopped. The only parking place near the hotel was in front of a hydrant and I remember thinking quite virtuously: "It won't cost the owner anything. They won't fine *him* because a thief parked his car on a hydrant."

I was tickled with myself for getting back to the hotel without being picked up so I went up to the football club's suite to celebrate with a drink. I had just settled into an armchair when the phone rang. It was Pete with his Irish temper in full flame. "Where the hell have you been?" he yelled. "I'm down here at the ballpark looking everywhere for you and you're sitting up there drinking! And now somebody has stolen our car!"

I scratched my head, and tried to think. "Hey Pete, what sort of car were we driving?" He described it to me. I'd stolen my own car!

"Hey Pete, you'll find your car down here in front of the hotel." Then I added as a kind afterthought: "And you'd better get down here quick or you'll get a ticket. You're parked on a hydrant!"

Great days. Great nights. But always next morning we were up at half-past-seven and out after business again. Our drinking never got in the way of work.

Liquor is a defence when you're somewhere where you're bored. Four or five drinks will get you into the spirit of anything. About the only thing I've regretted since I stopped drinking is that sometimes I'm bored in company.

I'm against restrictions on drinking. Canadian provincial governments set up stupid restrictions about where you can buy liquor and when. In Florida, on the other hand, you can buy it seven days a week, twenty-four hours a day, and I haven't seen any more drunks there than anywhere else. Long before that disastrous Prohibition experiment, I said: "If you want to do away with the liquor problem make it *free*. Have pumps where everybody can help themselves. Take the profit angle out of it."

However, although I make no stand against liquor, the past twenty years have shown me that you can accomplish most things in life without it. If it were possible to "disinvent" it, I'd be in favor because of the misery it has caused. But you can't disinvent it, and you can't ban it. The most you can do is educate people about it.

Chapter 17

SECRETS OF SUCCESS
Honesty saves a lot of trouble

Mr. Pickering, we're getting towards the end of your story, and now we all know you a lot better. We've heard how you climbed in business and politics and some of the things that happened en route, and we've met and enjoyed some of the people *you* met and enjoyed.

When we started talking, I suggested that yours is a special story because you can look at the world through the binoculars of age and success. It seems a good time now to ask what you think of the world that you see through those binoculars. It's time to put a few of those simple-sounding questions that can only have complex answers. Questions such as: what have you learned from it all? What are the secrets of living to ninety and managing to keep your sanity, sense, and sense of proportion? And what rules or principles have you developed or discovered for success in life and in business?

Let's talk about the business lessons first:

WHAT ARE THE BUSINESS LESSONS? I can only oversimplify them. Success in business involves figuring out at least three things: how to handle people, how to handle money, and how to handle your conscience. Plus, unavoidably a fourth all-purpose-magic-ingredient: luck.

"Handling" people may sound a bit like "manipulating" them, but it doesn't have to be all that negative. I was a manipulator when I persuaded Gerry LaFortune to take over Modern Building Cleaning. (I told him: "If you won't do it I'll have to; and it will *kill* me.") I'm sure Gerry has never regretted *that* manipulation. I was being a manipulator when I led Mackenzie King to release government property for the Lord Elgin. I played every angle I could think of to get him to do what I wanted, but it resulted in something he wanted to achieve too. The secret of handling — or "manipulating" — people is to understand what *they* want out of life in order to make that work for you.

No individual *knows* what skills he possesses until someone else puts him to the test. If you curb a man so that he has no opportunity to discover his abilities, he never develops confidence. A "manipulating" employer can *help* him. I've developed a lot of people a long way beyond what they considered their natural ability and they have had richer lives as a result. When I started manufacturing cleaning supplies I chose an ordinary workman, Johnnie McCauley, to run the plant and he soon left me standing as far as knowledge of that type was concerned. If I hadn't picked on him he may well have remained an ordinary laborer. Sometimes I went too far and pushed people to the point where they couldn't maintain their position. When this happened I adjusted things later so that they could find their level.

There are two types of men whose talents are wasted. One has ability he hasn't discovered; the other knows he has ability but is surrounded by other problems — such as lack of money or credit — so he can't go to work and make use of it.

A characteristic of the businessman is that he *employs* people. If I can get someone else to do something that I want done then I can make headway three or four times faster than if I try to do everything myself. That's why, throughout my career, even though I've always had several business balls in the air and at the same time have been deep into politics and public life, I've never been short of time to do the other things I wanted to do. My objective was always to work myself out of a job so I could go fishing or go to the track.

The other characteristic of the businessman is that when he employs other people he tries to make a profit on their efforts and this is what upsets left-wingers; they say that the profit one man makes on another's efforts is "exploitation". There's enough truth in what they say that it has to be thought through very carefully by any entrepreneur who's building for permanence and is not just an in-again-out-again operator.

My son-in-law tells me I get a lot of mileage out of people and I think it's true. People *have* worked very hard for me and I have gained by their efforts, but I tried very hard not to hurt them, and that's not as simple as it sounds.

Johnnie McCauley and many others stayed with me all their lives. They stayed because we treated them as human beings. I only paid the going wage rates, but they always felt I was their *friend;* they didn't *want* to work for anybody else. In return I still do everything I can for all those employees. They know that, while I still have a dollar, nothing can happen to them. As each of them retired, Gerry and I figured out how much each would need to live properly and then we fixed a life income to augment his pension. That approach creates loyalty, and an investment of that type pays terrific dividends.

I treated all my old-timers in that way but, with seven thousand employees now, we can't take quite the same care. The traffic wouldn't bear the expense. And yet I feel that somehow we should be *forced* to find a way to do it because many contribute their life's efforts to our company.

Being in possession of capital gives me no special right to take advantage of people. I can't be permitted to "use" a man all his life then throw him into the discard. I don't care that capitalism legally permits me to do that; I won't go that far with the system. Sure I'm as glad as the next man to make money, but I don't want money that tastes like that. I also want to be able to live with myself.

Once you have credit or capital it's not difficult to make more money because then you can make a fair capitalist's bargain which works as follows.

When I ask a young man to work with me, I contribute my credit. The young man says: "You put in your money and credit and maybe your know-how, and I'll put in my youth, my health, and my ability. Now we have a partnership." That's our bargain. Each contributes his assets. But, forty years later, what has happened? In terms of our original contributions the young man is now "bankrupt". His health, youth, energy, and ambition are all gone. May I then say: "This man can no longer fulfil our agreement. I must discard him"? May I forget the value he has left behind, that has passed into my hands? Could anything be more unfair? That man has left me assets for years and years to come, but *he* is now bankrupt. Capitalism says that I can discard him now with a clear conscience because I have "paid" him for his efforts. But *did* I pay him? *Can* you pay a man for his whole life? Leo McCauley, Johnnie's brother, retired the other day. He'd spent fifty-two years with Dustbane, starting as a laborer, working his way to supervisor of manufacturing; fifty-two years helping *me* to make money. On the day of his retirement party I stared at him a long time, wondering how a company can possibly pay a man for all those years. Finally I asked him: "Did you make a mistake, Leo, working for me all that time?"

"Mr. Pickering," he replied, "nothing would replace it." Leo was content; but I say that, under those circumstances, the capitalist has a remaining huge responsibility. He must make sure that such a man has security for the rest of his life; that, within reason, he has everything he needs. That's the debt and you haven't paid him until you finish the job.

We have never had a strike among Dustbane employees, but, as the company has grown bigger and less personal, the chances of a strike become greater. However, when a union makes unreasonable demands in any building we're cleaning, I always recommend to Gerry: "Pay what they ask. But cancel the contract for that building as soon as we can." We do a good job at a fair price with a fair profit; when the union prices us out of that we walk away.

So much for "handling people". Now for "handling money".

I've always taken the greatest care to keep a good relationship with banks — especially the Toronto-Dominion with which I've done the majority of my business. Since that one time when I put a foot out of line by using my current credit to rebuild the plant that burned down, I've been meticulous in how I use the bank's money. I've never hesitated to borrow — up to a half-million dollars at a time — but I was always conscious then that I was using the bank's money and wasn't free to do exactly as I pleased with it. The same feeling prevailed after we became a public company and paid off the bank. I told our senior people: "We've only traded masters. Before it was the bank; now it's the stockholders." There is always someone we're accountable to.

About a year ago I called in on the chairman of the TD bank and said: "Mr. Lambert, forty years ago, Mr. Lamb who was then president of this bank said, 'If you ever want any advice you have an invitation to come here any time.'" Mr. Lambert said: "Mr. Pickering, that invitation never will be rescinded. According to our records for forty years this has been the most pleasant relationship."

It seemed a good day for speeches so I added: "Mr. Lambert, my wealth is in what you have just said. More than anything I've accomplished, more than anything I possess, I would like to retain and deserve that reputation. I've made money, but my most valuable asset is my reputation."

Handling my conscience? All the evidence I've studied since I ran away from home eighty years ago indicates that honesty is the best policy. There's precious little chance of getting anywhere worthwhile by being even mildly dishonest. A policy of automatic, unquestioning honesty puts you on safe ground and you don't wake up each night wondering whether next day your sins will find you out and the ceiling collapse on you.

It takes as much effort to plan things a crooked way as to plan them the honest way. I can't be *bothered* dealing with crooks, or fishing in dubious waters. Honesty is a lot less trouble. I've often said that, if dishonesty paid I'd be dishonest, but it has always seemed obvious that the shifty way is also the stupid way. Jack Udd had problems with crooked politicians everywhere until he came to Ottawa. He was so surprised to find that C.E. Pickering wasn't on the make he later put me on the board of his company. After that over the years I made a lot of money with Udd; so I had the best of both worlds.

There's rarely been pressure on Dustbane or Modern Cleaning to do anything dishonest. One day my manager in Quebec City informed me that the civil servant in charge of a huge government contract there had said we should increase our invoices by five percent and refund the extra to him. My manager asked: "What shall I tell him?"

"There's only one answer," I replied. "And next time, if you don't know what that answer is, don't call me up to ask. Just call up to resign."

There are plenty of good selfish reasons behind my insistence that our people always be honest with our suppliers and customers. If I let our people feel it was smart for Dustbane to be dishonest with others, they'd have to believe it was equally smart to be dishonest with me. It's far more profitable for an organization to take total external and internal honesty for granted. I don't want to lie awake nights trying to figure ways to defend myself against employees who want to defraud me.

The fourth business essential is luck. On the day that Dustbane went public there was a little ceremony and, as the underwriter handed me a cheque for $2,300,000, someone asked me the standard secret-of-your-success question. "Ninety-nine-point-nine percent has been pure damn' luck," I told them. "And if you think I'm just being modest, let me prove to you how it is." I then skimmed through my career from the time that Gleason picked me to be a salesman. I listed all the instances where someone else's decision led to my success. "Now," I asked, "wasn't it mostly just luck?"

My other basic philosophy in business is that I am entitled to a profit. I have never wanted to get into cut-price selling. I tell a customer: "Mr. Brown, I'm not going to pretend I will sell you something for less than it cost me, because I won't. And the true cost includes a profit. That *belongs* to me." I say: "You can look over my books and see my profit. It's always about eight percent before taxes."

Of course I have to let that philosophy apply to the other fellow too. My wife was bragging one day that she had shopped around at a farmer's market until she had persuaded a man to sell her a chicken for fifty cents. I said she should have paid him a dollar. "How can he grow a chicken for fifty cents?" I asked. "If you pay him the dollar that it's worth then he will have money to buy more at the store and the store will have money to buy more Dustbane." It's no deal to buy something for less than it's worth. (Henry Ford may have said that better, but I said it last!)

Not everyone sees things my way. Some customers refused to sign cleaning contracts with Modern when they found they could get the job done cheaper elsewhere. Many of them however, returned later and asked us to take over. They'd learned that they're better off getting a good job at a fair price than a poor job at a cheap price.

There is one further fundamental of success. You have to *work*. You have to give it your best. You can't get licked in a deal then just sigh and walk away. When the pressure is on you have to stay there and meet it. You can't walk away until the pressure is *off*. Lots of people can't face up to that.

Chapter 18

CAPITALISTS' MISTAKES
Shame on some who don't think

You've convinced me well enough that "honesty pays" in business, especially if a man doesn't want to ruin his life by having to feel apprehensive or guilty all the time. But you haven't convinced me that all or even most businessmen see it that way. All sorts of enterprises in this society seem to do very nicely by selling shoddy goods; by advertising with those half-truths that half-lie; by setting up such sucker-bait schemes as pyramid selling. Your new American company is essentially a franchising company and it seems to offer a fair deal to the young men who join you — but there have been some awful semi-frauds perpetrated in franchising.

I don't believe that business has been anything like as scrupulous as you're suggesting it should be. And now the consumerism movement has surfaced in North America to question the very foundations of capitalism simply because millions of people believe that business is not sufficiently scrupulous. Are you the only good apple in the basket?

CAPITALISM HAS BAD ASPECTS. I'm a capitalist. I practise capitalism and I profit by it. Yet there are many aspects of the system that I don't subscribe to at all. I've gone along with it because, in North America, capitalism sets the rules of the game; and, during my working life, I've played the game according to those rules and I've won. But I'd change some of the rules if I could because, although I believe that capitalism is the best system man has found, it's still far from perfect. I'm disgusted, not with the system perhaps, but with the way many capitalists misuse and abuse it. This disgust has been coming on me for thirty or more years now, and lately it has become almost an obsession. (I have to watch myself or I will get people in a corner and bore them about it.)

The Watergate scandal was nothing new. That sort of thing and lots worse have been going on for years, with greedy politicians mixing in with greedy capitalists. Too many businessmen and politicians feather their own nests and seldom think of the common good. Yet, if more of us made more of a point of worrying about the good of all, we could transform society. We excuse our apathy or selfishness by saying: "You can't change human nature." But men finally got rid of the Spanish inquisition, didn't they? And debtor's prison? And slavery? Things do get improved with effort.

The genius of the private enterprise system is that it harnesses selfish motives for the public good and essentially it works well if we don't use it to exploit people. If we want to retain it — and presumably we capitalists do because we're the ones who have profited most by it — we must conduct ourselves with greater conscience. I feel frustration and fury when I see my fellow businessmen following unethical policies that can only lead to the *destruction* of the system we have all prospered under. Some people's business philosophy is to take advantage every time they can; those people are helping capitalism commit suicide.

Recently, for example, there's been a lot of talk about increasing interest rates to stop inflation. Banks say to their customers: "You now have a million dollars credit. If we allow you another $100,000 of purchasing power, you will make a greater demand on available supplies and that will automatically shove prices up. Therefore we will curb you by increasing the interest rate on the credit we've already extended to you. That will be a brake on this evil of inflation."

Now what are they really saying? "Instead of giving you this extra $100,000, we're going to charge you more for what you've got." Does that make sense? They hand you that then say: "Now you swallow it." I actually heard one banker on television say that he's putting up interest rates "for the good of society". That man *knows* he is a fake, a liar — he is putting that extra one percent straight into his pocket — but he has such contempt for the people that he is sure he will get away with it. I'm not against interest: money *has* a value, and people who lend it deserve a return. But how the devil can increasing the interest rates be "for the good of the people who pay it"! Statements like that are attempts to capitalize on foolishness.

Capitalists' mistakes

We must *improve* capitalism. We must cherish and improve anything that works because, God knows, the world has suffered under enough systems that don't work. If we businessmen want the benefits of capitalism we must prove we're entitled to them because, if we use the system to abuse people then, just as in Russia, the people will take the benefits away from us. I'm strongly against those outlaws who risk the entire system for their immediate and particular profit and it is we capitalists who should gang up against such pirates for our own protection. Even at ninety-two I'm ready right now to start a crusade against them. A lot of businessmen are conscious of this need but don't know how to start changing things.

It was the *evils* in Russia in the years before Communism that paved the way for what happened there. Are *we* doing something similar here? Is our stupidity going to bring about something we don't want? There's just no point in businessmen hogging things to the point where we destroy ourselves. It's surely better to have a little than to have nothing.

As a businessman, a capitalist, I always wanted more than success. I wanted my self-respect too. I wanted both and I got both. I believe that capitalism as a system can want and have both too. When capitalism is properly practised, businessmen can eat their cake and others can have it too, because capitalism *creates* wealth. It is, quite literally, creative, synergetic. That's the special magic in the system.

There's a myth that, under capitalism, management and labor are inevitably opposed. It's not true. Management and labor share the same boat. I understand the concerns of labor because, as a child, I saw the real evils inflicted on workers who had no union protection. The life of the working man then was awful. Families worked twelve hours a day and yet, at the end of every month, their debt to the company store was still more than they'd earned. It was a form of slavery. The unions came to grips with all that.

Henry Ford was the first to appreciate how richer workers can create richer employers, how raising standards for the workers creates a mass market for the capitalists' products. In 1914, when Ford cut the working day from nine to eight hours and offered his workers five dollars a day, half the world thought he was mad while the other half stormed his factory looking for work and had to be driven off with a firehose. Ford said it was better to make fifteen thousand families happy than to make a few people millionaires. He did both and *that* illustrates the true creativity of properly practised capitalism.

Today's automatic antagonism between union and management is destructive. Capital and labor together create wealth. At Dustbane we take raw materials and labor, mix a little with a lot, and come out with a product that we sell to earn money for us all. Everybody involved has an equity in what we create and, hopefully, there's a fair division of that equity. Even if labor gets three-quarters of it or more, I can still make a profit. I can analyze the products of *any* business and tell you what fairly belongs to the respective groups that helped create them. My only difficulty would be in setting a fair compensation, acceptable to labor, for the contribution of the "executive".

The man who works at a machine eight hours a day has no idea of the contribution made by the man who works with his head. The executive may play golf, drive a car, go to the races, yet still truly be "working". I might produce more wealth for Dustbane and its employees and shareholders with one thought than the man at the machine produces in a lifetime. What's the fair price for that thought, for the extra wealth it's created? I don't know. Yet I'm sure that, if reasonable men made the effort, they could figure it out, and surely that would be better than labor and capital continually fighting each other and partly destroying themselves in the process.

Alright, you say, C.E. Pickering can *see* all that and *say* all that but did he make it work in his own company? When Dustbane was small I was able to do it. Everybody associated with me then was treated according to the philosophy I had worked out. But it was harder to make it work in a large way and at times in later years, even at Dustbane, labor and management substituted antagonism for communication.

It's hard to fathom what some capitalists feel about the people who work for them. I remember a man named Cruickshank who was very active in the Canadian Manufacturers Association. I quite liked him although he was rather an "aristocratic" type which didn't meld very well with my background. He called me one day for a ride to a CMA meeting at Brockville and, driving down, we discussed the matter of working hours because the Ontario Government was about to cut the fifty-four hour work week down to forty-eight. I told him about an experience when I'd once had trouble getting orders out at my factory. At the time I'd remembered, from my East Blackstone childhood that my grandfather would never work a tired horse. A human being, I had mused, is at least as temperamental as a horse; maybe these sixty people in my plant are *tired*. Next day I told the foreman to call everybody together. "Boys," I announced, "starting next Monday we're cutting back to a forty-eight hour week, but your pay will stay the same. Just get out what orders you can." Within three weeks we had caught up on all orders and I never had that problem again. The shorter work week changed the spirit of the place.

I told Cruickshank that story yet, at the luncheon, he stood up and made a long speech *against* the forty-eight hour week. He moaned that it was a bad thing to "coddle the worker" and spouted a lot of other nonsense. By the time he had finished I was boiling mad and ready to refute him with my story. However another man jumped up even quicker than I could and told of his experience which had been similar to mine. His specific example easily offset the generalized fussing of the more conservative industrialist.

Now Cruickshank was a decent and honest man. I don't think he felt he was *against* the worker. He just didn't understand; and nor do many of the people who employ labor.

There's no difference between me and the man in my plant, except that I inherited some fortunate characteristics: imagination, ambition, determination to make something a reality. In every other respect he's the same as I am. Can I say that he is *inferior* to me? I can't sing a note; does that make me *inferior* to the opera singer? It's the capitalist who feels *superior* to other people who causes so much unnecessary trouble.

As I've already said, my concern at ninety-two is that the system will destroy itself because capitalists are so busy taking advantage of others. I ran into a perfect example the other day.

Main source of income for Florida banks is tourists and retired people. Suddenly the banks announced that they would no longer accept drafts on New York banks without a five-to-fifteen day delay to "transfer the funds". The average person doesn't know much about banking and probably thinks that some messenger carries his draft to New York, picks up the money, then returns. But of course there is no "transfer of funds" and there never was. It's all just bookkeeping. While those banks pretend that they're waiting for your money to "come from New York", they have the profitable use of it — and in Florida that can mean millions of dollars. When I protested this to the president of the Miami bank that I use, he didn't even try to justify the action. He simply immediately put through a memorandum that "Mr. Pickering does not have to wait until his funds are transferred from New York". But most people don't protest and the banks get away with it. They gouge the very segment of the public that creates their welfare. They're so stupid; it may take a few more years yet but people will eventually wake up to all such antics. And it's "people" who are always in the majority, not bankers or businessmen. The greed and unfairness of those banks helps drive us straight toward communism.

Capitalism has bred some crazy myths. Money itself is a myth, and we're slaves to it. During World War II, I sat at some official luncheon beside the editor of *The Christian Science Monitor*. He said to me: "The Allies will win the war if they don't run out of money."

I said: "You mean the Allies will win the war if they don't run out of red ink!" He looked at me for a minute then said: "You're right." There's never any *money* involved, only bookkeeping and there are no limits to the numbers you can put in books. Money is merely a symbol, yet people take it seriously. There isn't enough real "money" in Canada to take care even of Eaton's daily business. At Dustbane we do thirty-two million dollars' worth of business a year and the only actual *money* we see is the bit in petty cash.

We're stupid in the way we let ourselves be hampered by a so-called lack of money. When a community needs a hospital, obviously it has the materials and manpower it needs to build it, yet often that hospital doesn't get built because, they say, "we don't have the *money*". In reality, however, they can go ahead and build that damned hospital any time they like. Maybe they need to adopt the Social Credit idea and issue money backed by the community's new asset in the hospital. *However* they do it, there is a way. Lack of *money* need never stop us.

Some of that thinking is pretty close to Social Credit's "funny money" approach and I realize that such schemes are rarely as plausible as they sound. But every idea is worthy of study and, at a time when there is so much nonsense in the world, and when people go hungry because brilliant mankind has created shortages that didn't exist in the first place, then the least we can do is study alternatives that may have something to offer.

When I was sixty I voted for the first time in a Canadian election. I've always voted since then, until last year when I refused to because I am so fed up with the mess that our federal politicians — who are all basically capitalists — have made of our system. Sometimes my grandchildren argue with me on behalf of the New Democratic Party which is the closest Canada has to a Socialist party. Each time my fellow-capitalists demonstrate another example of self-serving stupidity, I almost think I could vote NDP myself.

Chapter 19

LESSONS OF LIFE
Don't hate, don't hurt, don't quit

We've come to the last chapter, Mr. Pickering.

That is, we have come to the last chapter of this book; not, from the look of things, to the last chapter of your life. We shouldn't tempt fate, I suppose, but it seems you will live a few more chapters yet. You certainly haven't stopped working and planning for the future. You've told us about a new business that may gross a hundred million dollars a year by the time you're a hundred. Within the last year, you have bought your first racehorses and now, very typically, you're showing a *profit* on them! I'm told that, one morning recently, you awoke at half-past-five in Miami, caught the seven o'clock flight to Toronto, connected to Ottawa, put in a day at the office, talked business all evening, then flew back to Miami at midnight, completing a twenty-three-hour day which, if I may say so, isn't bad for a ninety-two-year-old. There seems a fair head of steam in your boilers yet.

However, even though you still have some living to do, this *is* the last chapter of this book, and that's an obviously appropriate place to ask what you've learned from it all.

But, before we do that, let's acknowledge one thing: by any definitions I can think of, you're "a success". What can that mean?

You don't believe in gods or supermen, and you've discovered that heroes are few, so "success" doesn't have to indicate some superhuman achievement. You're obviously a physiological success because you've lived a long life in good health. You're a business success because the company you started in a whisky barrel is today worth twenty million dollars or so. As a human being you're "a success". That's proved by the love of the people who urged you to co-operate with me on this book.

So, "Mr. Success," let's ask it again: what have you learned from it all? What can you tell us about life? You've seen it from the bottom and from the top and you've lived it for fifty-two years more than I have. So what's the message? Is the world cruel or kind, hopeful or doomed, wise or stupid? Should I look forward to my next fifty-two years? Should your great-great-grandchildren be glad they've been born?

THERE IS A MESSAGE. On my ninetieth birthday they gave me a party and asked for a speech and I said: "I can't tell you how to live so long, but I do know one thing that's important: get rid of hatred and bitterness. Don't let it into your system. Hatred is a killer." So that's one thing I've learned.

When I hear of someone who dislikes me, I try to avoid the natural reaction, which is to decide that I dislike him too. Instead I try to tell myself that he may have reason to feel that way about me, and that I'd better take stock of myself and see what I'm doing wrong. In this way I try to immunize myself to resentment. Nobody can make me hate him: why should I govern *my* behaviour by *his* behaviour? People dominated by hatred get a lot of misery out of life and I feel that the lack of it has helped me live to ninety.

In business too, I've tried not to feel resentment against people who have resisted me. That's perhaps the one useful thing I learned from those New Yorkers; they hack and fight and backstab, but never hold a grudge.

In the last thirty years I've made an effort to keep my mind open, to avoid taking things for granted. That's harder to do as you grow older, but sometimes I think I've accomplished it. One day I was with a younger friend of mine, a man of about seventy, in discussion with a group of so-called "hippies". My friend and they debated and I listened. Finally I said to them: "If I were forced to choose the viewpoint of one of you over the other, I'd have to choose the attitude of you young barefooted people. You don't have all the answers, but at least you know that there are still many questions." My seventy-year-old friend, you see, felt that there are no more big questions, that the answers have all been found. I can tell you there are just as many questions nibbling at this ninety-year-old as at any child of four.

The one word that still preoccupies me is: why? Throughout life I was continuously impressed — and depressed — by the difficulty of getting intelligent answers to questions that don't seem all that difficult on the surface. Most people don't want to undertake serious thinking. Perhaps thinking is not pleasant. Why else have humans failed to arrive at more intelligent answers?

Why do people take such pleasure in destroying themselves, in going to war? Sometimes I find myself wondering: is it somehow *planned*, in some unknown cosmic scheme, that people *should* be miserable? Is there some mysterious logic in our being our own worst enemies? Warfare has been going on since the dawn of civilization, and we still endure and even enjoy these orgies of legalized murder. What is the reason for it? Is there a tension, a warfare, built right into the unfolding of the universe. There's surely tension and struggle in the seedling that, as it grows, splits open a rock. There's incessant warfare between animal species that feed on each other. Is there something constructive in all this struggle that we cannot sense? Otherwise, why do we continue to do it? We *know*, surely, that all these things men seem to be fighting for, would be easily available if they used their intelligence and not brute force in order to get them. Can't one group of men have their own type of society without interfering with the other fellow's? For example, I don't particularly want to be an American. I don't altogether like the American philosophy or way of life. But if I don't like it I don't have to try to sell them on my way of thinking. I can simply mind my own business. Why should I try to change Americans? If it's their way and they like it, why shouldn't they have it?

Human beings have a tendency to fool themselves, to substitute action for thinking. Since I was born there have been a million improvements in material things: electric lights, telephones, atomic power, aeroplanes, radio, television, rockets. But what good is all that stuff? We remain disturbed and confused and now, in addition, we're disturbed and confused and going at a speed that's ridiculous. Now we're disturbed by what's going on *everywhere*. In the past we didn't care what was happening in Europe or China. Today we are as aware of their problems as of our own. Eighty years ago in New England we had no electricity, radio, telephones, yet we still had a good life. We may even have been *more* content because few people ever moved more than five miles away from where they began. When someone was sick the neighbors did the nursing, and gave him the best of care. When someone was destitute he was looked after by the local people. When a man died he was laid out by the people; neighbors made the coffin and dug the grave. There was a spirit then that's lacking today. In our big cities today a girl can be raped with half-a-dozen people looking on and none raise a hand to stop it. I don't think we had callous people like that ninety years ago. Did we?

For all of our alleged human brilliance there isn't a thing we ever *created*. Everything was there from the beginning of time, waiting for us to "discover" it. We're not smart: we're *stupid* because it took us so long. Similarly, if you came back here in a hundred years, you'd see all sorts of things that it is possible for us to have today but that we're still too stupid to perceive.

In the millions of years of the world's existence each human being lives for only a flash, yet we spend most of our time on earth planning ways to make ourselves miserable. If people *tried,* they could solve most of the problems that bug mankind, but they're all too busy chasing illusory things. We share the world with tens of millions of people who are starving yet we, in our startling wisdom, pay farmers to keep their lands idle. Some of the best minds in Washington are occupied by the nonsense of wiretapping and other conspiracies to warp democracy instead of working on the problem of how to ship surplus food to hungry countries. Why does humanity inflict on itself so many things that make it unhappy?

If life is a mystery, it is also a game — which I play by the same rules as the others. I've been lucky in this game. Nothing bad has happened to me. But others haven't all been as lucky, and I hate to think of the misery heaped on them that could have been avoided by the use of intelligence.

I have been happy and I am happy now. You think perhaps that is because I have money? I'm not convinced of that. The prosperity I have attained is not essential to me. My so-called "wealth" has been mostly frozen in machinery and buildings anyway. There's not much I want to spend it on. I live modestly.

Making a few million dollars is no special achievement. I have a very dear friend, Peter Koch, a retired aero engineer from New York. One day he seemed depressed and he said to me: "I'm a failure." I think he was comparing his assets to those I have built up. "What are you talking about!" I demanded. "A failure as what? As an opera singer? Yes. As an outstanding businessman? Yes. But as a *man*? Among all the people I know, there is no finer man than Peter Koch. You've paid your bills, you've worked hard, you've supported your family, everybody likes you, you're honest. How can you say you're a *failure*? I can't sing opera either, so am I a failure?"

The only thing that really counts is whether you get by without hurting others. If you want to convince me that anything else is a sin you'll have to do so on the basis of logic. Almost everything that's labeled "sin" is merely something to do with protecting a system. Different parts of the world have different ideas of "sin" because they have different systems to protect.

I am not a religious man and, for all the generations that I know of, my ancestors have never been church people. I'll wait until the churches stop feuding before I join one. Because Stella was a Christian Scientist, I went to their services for years. But I didn't "join" her church because I knew I couldn't possibly live up to Christian Science ideals. Besides, they are vehemently anti-Catholic — and it's their anti-this-or-that-ness that puts me off all churches.

However, even though I personally have no feeling about God, I don't believe you can categorically *refute* anything. When Christian Science claims that all life is a dream from which one day we'll awake to reality, I don't say that's crazy. I just say that I don't know. My grandfather quite logically believed the earth was flat, but he would have been wrong to deny the possibility of it being round. We're wrong to deny any possibilities. TV seemed "impossible" for my first fifty years.

While admitting that we can't deny any possibilities, I still think it's important that parents encourage children to reason to the limits of their ability. We must educate individuals who will take the responsibility to think themselves out of the messes we older people have got us into. The day is past when parents can say to children: "This is the truth." Today's children simply reply: "Show me your proof." A couple of years ago I told the students at Ashbury College: "Use your God-given intelligence to do the job that we adults have failed to do. Work at it. Don't let apathy destroy you."

What will a society of people trained to overcome apathy do about the social inequality that man so far has been unable to escape? How will they reconcile the gap between rich and poor in every society? Will they decide, perhaps, that men are born equal in rights, but not in abilities, nor energy? Will they decide that it is just for some abilities to let you make money. Today's society doesn't question the fact that one man can have exceptional ability in art; we feel no discomfort in heaping rewards on a Picasso, a Nureyev, an Olivier. But we are less sure today about the rightness of rewarding a man who's smart at getting things done. Society is still uncomfortable with the proposition: "C.E. Pickering has a better business head therefore it's reasonable that he should get rich."

A society won't have equal distribution of wealth as long as wealth is related to the ability to produce. However it *can* make sure that everybody has an equal opportunity at the start. Opportunity should not depend on an accident of birth and yet, despite our great North American wealth, people are still born into limitations. Our society has a shortage of doctors only because it takes money to become a doctor. If doctors are needed why shouldn't society pay for their education? I would happily see the government invest any amount of money and time on education, so society can say to every individual at twenty-one: "You've all had an equal chance so far. Now you're on your own and you're on your way".

Inherited wealth is an obstacle to this. I don't think that the right of inheritance is a sound one. I don't see why significant wealth should be handed down the line to others who didn't help earn it. I play by the rules so I take advantage of legal loopholes to avoid paying inheritance tax, but I still don't agree with the basic principle.

That opens up another matter that disturbs me. There are so many loopholes in all tax laws that you'd think they'd been deliberately written to favor the wealthy. You could run a Cadillac through these loopholes.

Why are those loopholes left? My suspicion is that a privileged class has enough power to steer the laws through. Government talks out of two sides of its mouth. It talks to the common man during elections, but looks after the privileged class while in office. The loopholes are left so that wealth can continue to be passed from generation to generation while keeping the public unaware this is happening. Sometimes you see the same privileges and class protection at work in major bankruptcies and financial scandals. The professionals, the big money managers, the rich get their money out; the smaller man, the layman, the poorer man takes the beating.

In general I don't think our tax levels are unfair. Obviously we have to be taxed to get the benefits we all want. I'm no keener than the next man to hand money to the government and, like everyone, I resent waste in government operations. I'm not sure, however, that money as such can indeed be wasted. It just circulates again and I, as a businessman, may get some of it. The real crime is in hoarding money. During the thirties, when people were starving, the rich in New York might spend $50,000 to throw a party. I didn't criticize that. When they put that money into circulation everyone might get some of it.

People are fascinated by money but, for someone like me, in the final analysis, money is not the incentive to work. You can't *stop* men like me working. Once we've passed a certain point we don't think of money as such. Certainly we value *profit*, but only as a gauge of whether or not an enterprise is successful. Wealth lets me avoid the Canadian winter, but in Ottawa or Miami my lifestyle is very similar to that of anyone else. I live quietly. I don't like grandeur. I don't appreciate the "deluxe". Gerry LaFortune enjoys traveling first class through life and he has certainly earned the privilege. His house across the street from my $40,000 home in Ottawa must have cost three or four times as much as mine. He has a second mansion in the country, whereas my Florida home is a three-bedroom condominium. But I'm uncomfortable in swept-up surroundings; I don't fit, I don't want that stuff. My wife was never interested in having an elaborate home either, although my children live pretty high. I live at my own level. Whether I can afford it or not, I'm not going to do anything I think is foolish. I sometimes think of Kipling's lines: "If you can walk with crowds and keep your virtue, or walk with Kings — nor lose the common touch. . . ." I hope I've kept my "virtue"; I hope even more that I've kept the "common touch".

Should a man look forward to his second fifty years? He most certainly should. Life gets richer as you get older. Ninety-two is the happiest year of my life so far. I get more out of things now than I ever did. When you're young you're so busy you pass up the real things.

Today I feel I can get closer to people than I once did. During my working career I was apt to antagonize. I was impatient when others couldn't think as fast as I could and that was unreasonable. Gradually I trained myself to respect other people who had different types of minds. I grew more tolerant. I could have used more tolerance in my early life.

The one bad thing about old age is that you miss your friends. All those men I worked and drank and fished with are dead now and I can't expect to find anybody to replace them. That leaves a man feeling lost. Something has gone out of his life. Lots of people are nice to me now but I have no real cronies any more, apart from Peter Koch, and even he's twenty years younger.

Sometimes I remember my great old friend Dr. Roach; we fished together for thirty-five years. On the very first day we went fishing, he took me to his club. We started out at daylight and I quickly realized I wasn't wearing enough clothes — it was snowing! — but he didn't complain so I didn't either. When we finally got back to camp at night I found he was wearing six layers of clothes. If I had complained and dragged him the six miles back to camp, our friendship may have ended before it began. He never knew I damn' near froze to death that day.

And *he's* dead now.

The idea of dying doesn't worry me. You reach the point where you accept it. I don't think it's going to be too bad. When death comes to someone of seventy or eighty it is no catastrophe. It's just one more personality that has been here and gone again.

I don't believe in surrounding death with elaborate ceremonial. When Stella died in Boston I went to the undertaker and picked out the plainest casket I could find because that was what she would have wanted. (The undertaker was so disgusted that at first he wouldn't sell it to me.) I sent her body to her family home in Maine and I didn't even attend the funeral ceremony; I was in another room at the time. Nor did I look at her in the casket. I've never seen her grave. There's no marker on it because in Christian Science there's no such thing as "death". That was what Stella believed and I accepted it.

At today's average funeral, the body's in the undertaker's parlor on exhibit, and then they take a plot of land (that would be better used to grow potatoes) and bury that human body. When I die, they're going to cremate me and they can take the ashes and do what they damn' please with them. They can please themselves whether they put me in a funeral parlor, but I want no members of the family there. People can visit; I don't object to them paying respect to the memory of an individuality. They can write their names in a book then go away. The casket will be closed. The ceremony? No preacher, no minister, just a professional singer who will sing five psalms. And then the crematorium. I don't want some minister who didn't know me in the first place, telling people what I was like. He would only say what he thinks is pleasant for people to hear, and I don't want to be made out as some saint. If people want to know what I was like they can read this book.

After death the personality has gone. Where has it gone to? What's happened? That's a mystery that will never be solved. We pull many things down to our level of understanding but there are certain things that are beyond our power.

No two personalities are alike. That's also something beyond our power of understanding. Where do these personalities come from? Who knows — but I can sense that it's something to do with the universe as a whole. Where did the rose come from? Where did the perfection in nature come from? It's beyond our power to understand.

When I was a young man in Vancouver a friend and I once passed an old folk's home. They were all sitting in their rocking chairs on a long verandah. My friend said to me: "How do those people feel to see young people like us going by full of life and enjoying everything? It must be awful." I said to myself at the time: "I wonder."

I know now that it wasn't awful. They saw us youngsters chasing all over the place, but they weren't envious because they'd done their chasing. They'd found a lot of answers that we had yet to learn. I know that now.

There are a lot of things I still don't understand, and never will. Yet somehow, strangely, hopefully, even without knowing what is to happen, I feel I can agree with the statement of one man who went down on the Titanic. He said: "Death is life's greatest adventure."